The Gingerbread Golem's Shadow

The Gingerbread Golem's Shadow

Matthew Petchinsky

The Gingerbread Golem's Shadow: A Study in Sweet Darkness
By: Matthew Petchinsky

Introduction

A Tale of Two Traditions

The holiday season is a paradoxical time of year. On the surface, it glimmers with the promise of joy, togetherness, and warmth. Families gather around roaring fires, sharing stories and treats, while homes are adorned with twinkling lights that chase away the encroaching darkness of winter. Yet beneath this cheerful veneer lies a much older and more enigmatic layer of tradition—a shadowy undercurrent of folklore steeped in mystery, cautionary tales, and the lingering fear of the unknown.

This duality between light and shadow, joy and fear, is not a coincidence but rather an integral feature of humanity's enduring celebration of winter. The dark, cold months of the year have historically inspired a mix of merriment and trepidation. For every story of Santa Claus and his benevolent gift-giving, there exists a tale of Krampus punishing the wicked. For every cheerful carol sung around a Christmas tree, there is a whispered legend of vengeful spirits who walk the icy earth during the solstice.

The Gingerbread Golem sits squarely at the heart of this dichotomy. At first glance, it is a whimsical figure, born from a child's tale or a baker's fancy. Its origins in the creation of gingerbread figures and houses seem harmless, even delightful. Yet a closer examination reveals a far more complex and haunting narrative—a confectionery construct that symbolizes both the sweetness of holiday cheer and the eerie specter of folklore's shadowy past.

The Duality of Celebration

The holidays have always been a time to confront contrasts. In the darkest days of winter, our ancestors created rituals to celebrate the return of light and life. These rituals often straddled the line between invoking joy and warding off fear. While modern traditions focus on giving and gratitude, many of their origins are deeply tied to survival, protection, and the thin veil between the mundane and the mystical.

The Gingerbread Golem epitomizes this balance. On one hand, it is a creation of joy, born from the sweet alchemy of sugar, spices, and imagination. On the other, it carries echoes of the golem archetype from Jewish folklore—a being fashioned from inanimate material and imbued with life. Like the traditional golem, the Gingerbread Golem embodies the tension between creator and creation, protector and destroyer, light and shadow.

Sweetness and Shadow

Consider the act of baking a gingerbread figure. It is an intimate process, blending precise measurements and creative flair. But what if, in the shaping of this figure, there lies a spark of intent—a desire for protection, companionship, or even retribution? In this sense, the Gingerbread Golem transcends its sugary origins to become something more—a living symbol of humanity's desire to control the uncontrollable, to bring life to the lifeless, and to find meaning in the dark corners of existence.

The Gingerbread Golem's story is not merely a holiday novelty but a lens through which we can explore broader themes. What does it mean to create something imbued with both sweetness and strength? Why do we, in the midst of celebration, feel drawn to stories that carry a hint of menace? These questions lead us to the heart of winter folklore, where joy and fear coexist in delicate balance.

The Shadowy Roots of Holiday Folklore

Winter folklore has always walked the line between light and darkness. From the Norse myths of Yule to the Central European legends of Perchten and Krampus, the stories we tell during the darkest days of the year often serve dual purposes: to entertain and to instruct, to delight and to caution. These tales remind us that while the holidays bring warmth and light, they also demand respect for the forces that lurk in the cold and dark.

The Gingerbread Golem, like many figures of winter folklore, straddles this line. It is both a protector and a potential threat, a creation of joy that carries an undercurrent of unease. Its sugary form and festive trappings belie a deeper, darker nature—a reminder that even in the most joyful celebrations, the shadows are never far away.

A Symbol of Duality

As we embark on this exploration of "The Gingerbread Golem's Shadow," we will delve into the many layers of meaning this figure represents. From its sugary sweetness to its uncanny strength, the Gingerbread Golem is a symbol of duality that speaks to the heart of the holiday season. Through its story, we can uncover the profound and sometimes unsettling truths that lie beneath the surface of our most cherished traditions.

This is a journey into the heart of the holidays—not just the light and laughter but also the mystery and shadows that make this season so deeply resonant. The Gingerbread Golem, standing at the crossroads of sweetness and darkness, invites us to embrace the complexity of our traditions and to find beauty in the balance between opposites.

Chapter 1: The Birth of Gingerbread: Sweet Origins and Bitter Roots

Gingerbread, that sweet and spicy confection we associate with holiday cheer, has a history as rich and complex as its flavor. Long before it adorned our tables as gingerbread men or intricately decorated houses, it held a deeper, almost mystical significance. Its story is one of transformation, rooted in ancient rituals, medieval medicine, and a symbolic relationship with the natural world.

To understand the true origins of gingerbread, we must journey back to a time when sugar and spice were not just luxuries but symbols of power, protection, and the sacred.

The Origins of Ginger and Its Mystical Allure

The story of gingerbread begins with its star ingredient: ginger. This aromatic spice traces its roots to ancient Asia, where it was prized not only for its culinary uses but also for its medicinal and mystical properties. In early Chinese and Indian cultures, ginger was believed to ward off evil spirits and disease. It was used in Ayurvedic medicine to treat ailments ranging from nausea to inflammation, and its warming properties were thought to invigorate the body and soul.

As trade routes expanded, ginger traveled westward, becoming a coveted commodity in ancient Greece and Rome. The Romans, in particular, viewed ginger as a powerful aid for digestion and incorporated it into their cooking and remedies. However, they also recognized its symbolic power, using it in ceremonies to purify spaces and protect against malevolent forces.

The First Forms of Gingerbread

The earliest iterations of gingerbread were far removed from the sweet, cookie-like treats we know today. In ancient Egypt, honey cakes infused with spices like ginger were offered to gods and buried with the dead to ensure safe passage to the afterlife. These cakes, often shaped into symbolic forms, were not merely sustenance but acts of devotion and protection.

In medieval Europe, ginger began to take on a more central role in culinary and ritualistic practices. Monks and nuns experimented with ginger as a preservative and a flavor enhancer, creating dense, spiced cakes that could be stored for long periods. These early "gingerbreads" were often used in religious ceremonies and festivals, where they were seen as sacred offerings.

Gingerbread also played a role in the medieval concept of humoral theory—the idea that the balance of bodily fluids determined health and temperament. The warming nature of ginger made it a prized ingredient during the cold, dark months of winter, believed to restore balance and vitality to the body.

Gingerbread as a Symbol of Power and Protection

By the late Middle Ages, gingerbread had evolved into a delicacy enjoyed by both commoners and royalty, though its significance went far beyond taste. Gingerbread was often shaped into intricate designs—animals, saints, and even architectural forms—that carried symbolic meaning.

In Germany, for example, Lebkuchen, a traditional form of gingerbread, was baked in molds depicting religious scenes or protective symbols. These gingerbread figures were believed to ward off evil, bless households, and bring good fortune during the harsh winter months.

Similarly, in England, Queen Elizabeth I is credited with popularizing the gingerbread man. Legend has it that she had cookies shaped like the courtiers of her court, gifting them as a sign of favor. While these treats delighted her guests, they also reflected the symbolic use of gingerbread as a representation of power and protection.

The Darker Roots of Gingerbread Rituals

Though gingerbread became a festive treat, its roots remained intertwined with darker, more ritualistic practices. In some cultures, gingerbread figures were used in folk magic and pagan rituals, where they symbolized human surrogates. Shaped into effigies, they were baked and broken as part of ceremonies meant to banish illness, misfortune, or malevolent spirits.

In parts of Eastern Europe, gingerbread houses—much like the ones we build today—were originally created as offerings to appease woodland spirits. These edible homes were thought to act as gifts, ensuring the spirits' favor and protection through the winter.

Even the Grimm Brothers' tale of "Hansel and Gretel" hints at the darker associations of gingerbread. The witch's gingerbread house, while enticing and sweet, is ultimately a trap—a stark reminder of the duality of gingerbread as both a symbol of comfort and a harbinger of danger.

The Sweet and the Sacred: Gingerbread's Transformation

As gingerbread transitioned from sacred offering to holiday tradition, its role in society shifted but never completely abandoned its symbolic roots. The Industrial Revolution brought about mass production, making gingerbread accessible to the general population. This democratization of the treat cemented its place as a holiday staple, but its association with protection and prosperity persisted.

Gingerbread houses became a popular holiday activity, rooted in German Christmas traditions but spreading worldwide. Though now a symbol of joy and creativity, the act of crafting a gingerbread house retains echoes of its ancient purpose: to bring warmth, cheer, and protection to the home during the long, dark winter nights.

Gingerbread in the Modern Age

Today, gingerbread is often seen as nothing more than a holiday indulgence. Yet, its rich history continues to resonate, even if subconsciously. The act of shaping gingerbread figures and houses taps into a deep, primal need for connection, creation, and protection. Whether we realize it or not, the Gingerbread Golem—a fusion of sweetness and strength, light and shadow—is a living symbol of this ancient tradition.

As we explore the tale of the Gingerbread Golem in the chapters to come, we will see how this seemingly simple confection embodies the duality of holiday traditions: the sweetness of celebration and the shadowy echoes of rituals long past. Gingerbread's journey from ancient offering to festive treat is not merely a story of culinary evolution but a testament to humanity's enduring need to find meaning and balance in the darkest days of the year.

Chapter 2: The Golem Archetype: Protector or Punisher?

The figure of the golem, a creature shaped from inanimate material and animated through mystical or divine intervention, has long captured the imagination of storytellers, theologians, and philosophers. Emerging from Jewish mysticism, the golem is both a protector and a potential punisher—a being of immense power yet bound by the will of its creator. This duality makes the golem an enduring archetype in folklore and a fascinating subject of philosophical exploration.

To understand the Gingerbread Golem as a modern iteration of this archetype, we must first delve into the origins of the golem myth, its symbolic meanings, and its evolution in contemporary culture.

The Origins of the Golem in Jewish Mysticism

The term "golem" originates from the Hebrew word **"golem,"** meaning "formless" or "unfinished." In the Talmud, it refers to an unformed substance, often used metaphorically to describe an incomplete or undeveloped being. However, it was in the mystical teachings of Kabbalah that the golem took on its more recognizable form as a creature molded from clay or earth and brought to life through sacred rituals.

The most famous golem tale comes from 16th-century Prague, where Rabbi Judah Loew ben Bezalel, the Maharal of Prague, is said to have created a golem to protect the Jewish community from persecution. According to legend, Rabbi Loew inscribed the Hebrew word **"emet"** (truth) on the golem's forehead to animate it. The golem became a tireless guardian, executing the rabbi's will without question. However, when the golem's power grew uncontrollable, it had to be deactivated by removing the first letter of "emet," leaving the word **"met"** (death).

This story captures the central tension of the golem archetype: a being created to serve and protect but capable of immense destruction if left unchecked. The golem's very existence raises questions about the responsibilities and limits of human creation.

The Golem as Protector

At its core, the golem is a symbol of protection. In a world rife with dangers—both physical and spiritual—the golem represents the human desire to create guardians capable of withstanding threats beyond our control.

1. **A Defender of the Marginalized**

   The golem's association with Jewish communities during times of persecution reflects its role as a protector of the vulnerable. Its loyalty and strength are unwavering, embodying the hope that justice and safety can prevail even in the face of overwhelming adversity.

2. **A Reflection of Divine Power**

   The golem is also a representation of humanity's connection to the divine. By shaping life from lifeless material, the creator of the golem mimics the acts of God, asserting both a sense of agency and humility. The golem is not a rival to divine creation but a tool through which the divine will is enacted.

3. **The Guardian of the Home**

   Beyond its role in communal protection, the golem archetype has also been interpreted as a personal guardian. In some folktales, golems are tasked with safeguarding homes, families, or sacred spaces, embodying the desire for security in an uncertain world.

The Golem as Punisher

While the golem is often a protector, its potential for destruction is an equally integral part of its identity. The same strength that makes it a guardian can turn it into a punisher, especially when its creator loses control or misuses its power.

1. **Unyielding Obedience and the Danger of Literalism**

   One of the golem's most notable traits is its inability to interpret nuance. It follows its creator's commands to the letter, which can lead to unintended consequences. For example, a golem tasked with protecting a community might use excessive force, punishing not only aggressors but also innocents caught in its path.

2. **The Creator's Hubris**

   The golem's destructive potential is often a reflection of the creator's hubris. In attempting to wield divine powers, the creator risks unleashing forces they cannot fully control. This theme is echoed in later myths, from Frankenstein's monster to modern AI narratives, where the creation becomes a threat to its creator.

3. **The Punisher of Injustice**

   In some tales, the golem acts as an avenger, punishing those who have wronged its creator or community. This role aligns with the archetype's connection to justice but also raises ethical questions about the use of violence and retribution.

The Golem in Philosophical Context

The golem archetype invites profound philosophical questions about creation, power, and morality.

1. **What Does It Mean to Create Life?**

   The act of creating a golem mirrors humanity's ongoing quest to shape life, whether through art, science, or spirituality. It challenges us to consider the ethical implications of creation: What responsibilities do we bear toward our creations? What limits should we impose on our ambitions?

2. **The Balance Between Protection and Autonomy**

   The golem's lack of autonomy raises questions about the nature of free will and servitude. Is a protector truly benevolent if it cannot choose its actions? How do we reconcile the desire for safety with the need for agency?

3. **The Shadow of the Creator**

   The golem's potential for destruction often reflects the flaws or fears of its creator. This dynamic underscores Carl Jung's concept of the shadow—the idea that the darker aspects of the self, if ignored or suppressed, can manifest in destructive ways.

The Golem in Modern Interpretations

The golem archetype has transcended its origins, appearing in a wide range of modern narratives.

1. **Literature and Film**

   From Mary Shelley's *Frankenstein* to the clay soldiers of *The Mummy*, the golem's influence is evident in countless stories of artificial beings. These narratives often grapple with the same themes of protection, punishment, and the limits of human ambition.

2. **Technology and Artificial Intelligence**

   In the digital age, the golem serves as a metaphor for the power and risks of technological creation. AI systems, like golems, are designed to serve but can cause harm if poorly programmed or misunderstood.

3. **The Gingerbread Golem as a Modern Reimagining**

   The Gingerbread Golem blends the traditional golem archetype with festive themes, embodying both the sweetness of holiday cheer and the shadowy potential for chaos. Like its clay predecessor, the Gingerbread Golem raises questions about the balance between creation and control, protection and punishment.

A Symbol of Duality

The golem archetype, with its dual role as protector and punisher, continues to resonate because it reflects the complexities of human nature. It is a mirror of our deepest desires and fears—our yearning for safety, our hunger for power, and our struggle to manage the unintended consequences of our actions.

As we explore the Gingerbread Golem in the context of this archetype, we will see how it encapsulates these timeless themes while adding a festive, yet haunting, twist. The golem's shadow looms large in folklore and philosophy, reminding us that even our most noble creations carry the potential for darkness.

Chapter 3: The Sweet Sentinel: Gingerbread as a Guardian Figure

The image of a gingerbread golem—crafted from flour, spices, and sugar, yet imbued with an air of magical authority—feels simultaneously whimsical and profound. At its heart, the concept of the Gingerbread Golem as a guardian figure taps into humanity's deep-seated need for protectors during times of vulnerability. The Gingerbread Golem, in its imagined role as the "Sweet Sentinel," represents the ideal fusion of festive joy and symbolic strength, embodying the protective spirit of the holiday season.

Origins of Gingerbread as Protection

To understand how gingerbread came to be viewed as a guardian figure, we must first examine its historical role in rituals and traditions. Gingerbread has long been intertwined with the concept of protection, serving as a talisman against misfortune, a blessing for the home, and even a shield against darker forces.

1. **Symbolic Strength in Spices**

   In medieval Europe, ginger and other spices were not only culinary luxuries but also considered medicinal and protective. Ginger's warming properties were thought to ward off the cold and sickness of winter, while cinnamon and clove were believed to purify the air and repel negative energies. When these spices were baked into gingerbread, the resulting treat became more than food—it became a symbolic shield of warmth and vitality.

2. **Edible Guardians for Sacred Spaces**

   Early gingerbread figures were often shaped into religious or protective symbols, such as angels, saints, or mythical creatures. These figures were placed in homes or given as gifts to convey blessings and ward off harm. In this way, gingerbread figures acted as spiritual sentinels, standing guard over the spaces they inhabited.

3. **The Gingerbread House as a Fortress**

The tradition of building gingerbread houses—rooted in German holiday customs—was not merely an artistic exercise but a symbolic act of protection. The gingerbread house, sturdy yet sweet, represented a safe haven against the harshness of winter and the potential dangers lurking in the dark. In some folklore, these houses were believed to shield families from malevolent spirits or bad luck during the cold months.

The Gingerbread Golem as Protector

The Gingerbread Golem, as a modern interpretation of these traditions, amplifies the protective qualities of gingerbread into a figure of strength and vigilance. By imbuing this confectionery construct with the attributes of a golem, we create a Sweet Sentinel—a being capable of defending holiday cheer against forces that seek to disrupt it.

1. **A Guardian of Festivity**
   The holiday season, with its emphasis on joy, family, and light, is paradoxically vulnerable to disruption. Stress, conflict, and even darker folkloric forces like Krampus or the Yule Cat can loom over the season. The Gingerbread Golem serves as a symbolic protector of the holiday spirit, standing as a cheerful yet powerful figure who ensures that the warmth of the season prevails.

2. **A Watchful Presence**
   Like its clay golem predecessor, the Gingerbread Golem can be imagined as a tireless guardian. Whether stationed at the hearth, a festive centerpiece on a table, or in the form of a towering gingerbread sculpture, this figure watches over its domain with silent resolve. Its sweet exterior belies its unwavering purpose: to shield its creators from harm and preserve the sanctity of holiday joy.

3. **The Act of Creation as Empowerment**
   The process of crafting a Gingerbread Golem mirrors the act of summoning a protector. From carefully kneading the dough to shaping and decorating the figure, every step carries an element of intent. Just as the golem's creator inscribed sacred words to animate it, so too does the baker infuse their creation with care, love, and purpose. The result is a sentinel whose strength is drawn from the spirit of its maker.

The Gingerbread Golem in Folklore and Mythology

The idea of a guardian figure crafted from humble materials is not unique to gingerbread. The Gingerbread Golem draws upon a rich tapestry of mythological and folkloric traditions in which protective beings are created to shield communities or individuals.

1. **The Protective Archetype in Winter Folklore**

   Winter has always been a time of heightened vulnerability, inspiring stories of guardians who ward off the dangers of the season. From the snow-covered mountains of Scandinavia to the forests of Eastern Europe, myths often feature protectors who stand watch against malevolent spirits and natural forces. The Gingerbread Golem fits neatly into this archetype, blending the festive charm of the season with the protective strength of a golem.

2. **The Power of Food as a Guardian Symbol**

   Across cultures, food has often been used as a protective symbol. In Hindu tradition, offerings of food are made to deities to invoke their blessings. In medieval Europe, bread was sometimes shaped into crosses or other sacred symbols to bless households. Gingerbread, with its long history as a sacred and celebratory treat, naturally lends itself to this role as an edible guardian.

3. **Modern Adaptations in Popular Media**

   The Gingerbread Golem, while not as widely recognized as other holiday figures, has begun to appear in modern storytelling. From animated films to festive fantasy novels, the idea of a living gingerbread protector has captured the imagination of creators. These adaptations often emphasize the golem's duality—its sweetness tempered by strength, and its festive charm contrasted with its potential for power.

The Sweet Sentinel's Symbolic Role

As a guardian figure, the Gingerbread Golem transcends its humble origins to become a symbol of hope, resilience, and community. Its presence represents the idea that even the most fragile and sweet things can possess great strength.

1. **Resilience in Fragility**
   The Gingerbread Golem embodies the paradox of strength in fragility. Though gingerbread is easily broken, its role as a guardian figure reminds us that strength is not always about physical durability. It is about the spirit of perseverance, the sweetness of intention, and the ability to protect what truly matters.

2. **Unity and Togetherness**
   The act of creating a Gingerbread Golem often involves collaboration, whether it's a family baking together or a community coming together to build a giant gingerbread sculpture. This collective effort reinforces the idea that protection and strength come from unity.

3. **A Reminder of Balance**
   The Gingerbread Golem also serves as a reminder of the balance between lightheartedness and seriousness. Its festive appearance brings joy, but its role as a sentinel speaks to the deeper need for vigilance and care during the holiday season.

Conclusion: The Guardian of Holiday Spirit

The Gingerbread Golem, as the Sweet Sentinel, is a powerful symbol of the holiday season's dual nature. It is a protector of joy, standing as a bulwark against the stresses and shadows that threaten to intrude upon festive celebrations. Yet it is also a reflection of the deeper themes of resilience, unity, and balance that define the season.

In its sugary form, the Gingerbread Golem reminds us that even the smallest, sweetest creations can carry the strength to protect and inspire. As we continue to explore its role in this study of sweet darkness, we will see how its presence bridges the gap between tradition and innovation, light and shadow, and sweetness and strength.

Chapter 4: The Shadows of Winter: Darkness in Holiday Folklore

The holiday season, characterized by twinkling lights, festive gatherings, and cheerful songs, is also a time of long, dark nights and harsh, unforgiving winters. Beneath the surface of joy and celebration lies a deeper, often unsettling undercurrent: the shadows of winter. Throughout history, these shadows have manifested in myths and folklore that remind us of the season's dangers and the delicate balance between celebration and survival.

This chapter explores the darker side of holiday folklore, from fearsome figures like Krampus to haunting legends of the Yule Cat, and examines where the Gingerbread Golem fits into this chilling tapestry.

The Dual Nature of Winter Folklore

Winter folklore often carries a dual message: it inspires joy and unity while also issuing warnings about the perils of the season. This duality reflects humanity's historical experience of winter as a time of scarcity, isolation, and vulnerability. To survive, communities created myths that reinforced social cohesion, encouraged generosity, and warned against transgressions that could threaten the fragile balance of life during the cold months.

1. **Celebration Amid the Shadows**

   Winter festivals, such as Yule, Saturnalia, and later Christmas, were established to bring light and hope to the darkest days of the year. Yet these celebrations often included elements of fear and caution, acknowledging that the season also brought danger—be it from the harsh environment, malevolent spirits, or human failings like greed and selfishness.

2. **The Role of Dark Figures in Folklore**

   Many winter myths include shadowy figures who serve as enforcers of morality, protectors of tradition, or harbingers of doom. These figures remind us that while the season is a time for joy, it is also a time to tread carefully, honoring the forces of nature and community.

Krampus: The Dark Companion

Among the most famous dark figures of winter folklore is Krampus, a fearsome, horned creature who serves as the counterbalance to St. Nicholas.

1. **Origins and Characteristics**

   Krampus originates from Alpine folklore, where he is depicted as a demonic figure with horns, a long tongue, and chains. He accompanies St. Nicholas, rewarding well-behaved children with gifts while punishing the naughty ones. Krampus might leave coal as a warning—or worse, carry misbehaving children away in a sack.

2. **Symbolism of Krampus**

   Krampus embodies the dual nature of the season: while St. Nicholas represents generosity and kindness, Krampus enforces discipline and fear. This balance ensures that the holiday is not only a time of indulgence but also a reminder of the consequences of poor behavior.

3. **Krampus in Modern Culture**

   In recent years, Krampus has enjoyed a resurgence in popular culture, appearing in parades, movies, and literature. This revival reflects a growing fascination with the darker aspects of holiday tradition and a recognition that joy is often heightened by a touch of fear.

The Yule Cat: A Feline Enforcer

The Yule Cat, or **Jólakötturinn**, is another fearsome figure of winter folklore, hailing from Icelandic tradition.

1. **The Legend of the Yule Cat**

   According to legend, the Yule Cat prowls the countryside during the winter, seeking out those who have not received new clothes for Christmas. Those who fail to meet this requirement risk being devoured by the monstrous feline.

2. **A Lesson in Generosity and Hard Work**

   While the Yule Cat may seem arbitrary in its judgment, its story served a practical purpose. In Iceland's harsh winters, ensuring that everyone had warm clothing was a matter of survival. The Yule Cat's legend encouraged people to share resources and work diligently during the year to provide for their families.

3. **The Yule Cat's Symbolic Role**

   Like Krampus, the Yule Cat serves as a reminder that holiday cheer must be earned through effort and generosity. It reinforces the idea that the season is not just a time for receiving but also a time for giving and preparing for the challenges ahead.

The Perchta and the Wild Hunt

In Germanic and Scandinavian folklore, the figure of **Perchta** and the myth of the Wild Hunt add another layer of shadow to the winter season.

1. **Perchta: The Belly-Slitter**

   Perchta, also known as Bertha or Frau Holle, is a figure associated with the Twelve Days of Christmas. She is both a giver of gifts and a punisher of the lazy. According to legend, Perchta rewards those who work hard and follow traditions, but she punishes the idle by slitting their bellies open and stuffing them with straw.

2. **The Wild Hunt**

   The Wild Hunt, a spectral procession of ghostly riders, is said to sweep across the winter skies, bringing misfortune to those who encounter it. Led by figures like Odin or Perchta, the Wild Hunt represents the chaotic, untamed forces of nature that are especially potent during the dark months.

3. **Lessons from Perchta and the Wild Hunt**

   These legends emphasize the importance of adhering to social norms and respecting the natural order. They also serve as a stark reminder of the consequences of neglecting one's duties during the winter.

The Gingerbread Golem: A New Figure in Winter Folklore

The Gingerbread Golem, while a modern invention, fits seamlessly into the tradition of dark winter folklore. Like Krampus, the Yule Cat, and Perchta, it embodies the duality of the season, acting as both a guardian and a potential punisher.

1. **A Protector of Holiday Spirit**

   The Gingerbread Golem's role as a Sweet Sentinel aligns it with the protective aspects of winter folklore. It stands guard over the holiday spirit, ensuring that joy and togetherness are preserved against the encroaching shadows of stress, greed, and discontent.

2. **A Symbol of Consequences**

   Like other shadowy figures, the Gingerbread Golem can serve as a reminder of the consequences of neglecting the values of the season. Its imposing presence warns against selfishness, waste, and disregard for the community, reinforcing the importance of generosity and gratitude.

3. **Blending Light and Dark**

   The Gingerbread Golem's sweet exterior and golem-like strength make it a perfect representation of the balance between light and dark in holiday folklore. Its sugary form invites warmth and creativity, while its potential for power reminds us of the seriousness underlying the season's traditions.

The Role of Shadows in Celebration

The dark figures of winter folklore, including the Gingerbread Golem, play an essential role in deepening our appreciation for the holiday season.

1. **Enhancing the Light**
   The presence of shadows makes the light of the season shine brighter. Knowing that winter is a time of danger and hardship helps us value the warmth, joy, and unity that the holidays bring.

2. **Teaching Valuable Lessons**
   Figures like Krampus, the Yule Cat, and the Gingerbread Golem teach lessons that go beyond morality tales. They remind us of the importance of preparation, hard work, and community in overcoming the challenges of winter.

3. **Fostering Resilience**
   By confronting the shadows of the season, we cultivate resilience. The knowledge that joy exists alongside darkness helps us navigate the complexities of life with greater strength and balance.

Conclusion: Where the Gingerbread Golem Fits

In the grand tapestry of holiday folklore, the Gingerbread Golem occupies a unique place. It combines the sweetness of modern holiday traditions with the strength and cautionary power of ancient myths. As a new figure in the shadows of winter, the Gingerbread Golem invites us to reflect on the dual nature of the season—where light and darkness, joy and fear, sweetness and strength coexist in perfect balance.

Through its story, we are reminded that the holidays are not just a time of celebration but also a time to honor the shadows that make the light so precious.

Chapter 5: Edible Effigies: Food as Symbol and Sacrifice

Food is one of humanity's oldest forms of storytelling. Beyond sustenance, food serves as a medium for symbolism, ritual, and connection to the divine. Throughout history, cultures have used edible creations—effigies of deities, animals, and mythical beings—to honor traditions, ward off evil, and forge connections with the natural and spiritual worlds.

Gingerbread, with its rich history and ritualistic origins, is a quintessential example of an edible effigy. In this chapter, we explore how gingerbread and other festive foods have been imbued with symbolic meaning, transformed into objects of ritual, and sometimes even offered as sacrifices.

The Origins of Edible Effigies

The concept of edible effigies—foods shaped into forms with symbolic significance—dates back to ancient civilizations.

1. **Offerings to Deities**

   Ancient cultures often created food effigies as offerings to their gods. In Egypt, honey cakes shaped like animals or sacred symbols were left in temples or buried with the dead as provisions for the afterlife. Similarly, in ancient Greece, bread and cakes shaped like wheat sheaves or animals were used to honor Demeter, the goddess of the harvest.

2. **Sacred Shapes and Seasonal Symbols**

   The act of shaping food into recognizable forms often carried seasonal or agricultural significance. For example, bread shaped like the sun was used in solstice celebrations to invoke the return of light during the darkest days of winter. These edible creations were both a celebration of life and an acknowledgment of the cyclical nature of existence.

3. **Consumption as Communion**

   Many traditions involved the ritualistic consumption of edible effigies, symbolizing communion with the divine or the natural world. Eating these foods was not merely an act of nourishment but a sacred ritual that connected the consumer to the forces they represented.

Gingerbread as a Ritualistic Food

Gingerbread, with its combination of aromatic spices and intricate shapes, evolved as one of the most enduring edible effigies in European traditions.

1. **Symbolism in Spices**

   The spices used in gingerbread—ginger, cinnamon, clove, and nutmeg—carried deep symbolic meanings. These spices were seen as warming agents, both physically and spiritually, capable of warding off illness and negative energies. Their exotic origins added an air of mystery and luxury, further enhancing gingerbread's significance.

2. **Early Rituals Involving Gingerbread**

   In medieval Europe, gingerbread figures were often crafted for specific rituals or celebrations. They were shaped into animals, saints, or mythical creatures, reflecting the beliefs and intentions of their creators. These effigies were used in processions, festivals, and religious ceremonies, where they acted as blessings or protective talismans.

3. **Gingerbread and the Seasons**

   Gingerbread became particularly associated with winter celebrations, where its warming spices and festive shapes symbolized the triumph of light and warmth over the darkness of winter. Baking gingerbread effigies during the cold months was a communal act of hope and protection, linking families and communities to the cycles of nature.

Edible Effigies in Holiday Traditions

Gingerbread is just one example of how edible effigies play a central role in holiday traditions worldwide.

1. **Yule Logs (Bûche de Noël)**

   The Yule log, originally a large piece of wood burned during winter solstice celebrations, was transformed into an edible cake in 19th-century France. Shaped and decorated to resemble a log, this dessert symbolizes renewal, warmth, and the return of light.

2. **Christmas Pudding and Hidden Charms**

   In England, Christmas pudding was more than a dessert; it was a symbolic ritual. Families would gather to stir the pudding, each person making a wish. Charms hidden inside the pudding, such as coins or rings, carried messages of fortune or luck for the finder.

3. **Sugar Skulls and Day of the Dead**

   In Mexico's Day of the Dead celebrations, sugar skulls represent deceased loved ones. These brightly decorated edible effigies honor the dead while celebrating the cycle of life and death. Like gingerbread, sugar skulls blend sweetness with profound spiritual significance.

4. **King Cakes and Ritual Sharing**

   King cakes, associated with Epiphany and Mardi Gras, are shaped into rings or crowns and often contain a hidden figurine. The person who finds the figurine is granted good fortune or tasked with hosting the next celebration. This tradition emphasizes community and shared responsibility.

The Sacrificial Aspect of Edible Effigies

While the idea of sacrificing food may seem outdated, the symbolic act of offering or consuming an edible effigy retains echoes of its sacrificial origins.

1. **Offering to Spirits and Deities**

   Many cultures believed that by offering food to gods or spirits, they could appease these forces and ensure blessings. Gingerbread effigies, placed on altars or shared during festivals, were thought to attract positive energies and protect against misfortune.

2. **Sacrifice as Gratitude**

   The act of baking and sharing edible effigies can be seen as a form of sacrifice—a way to give back to the earth or community. In medieval Europe, gingerbread was often given as a gift to express gratitude, strengthen bonds, or seek protection.

3. **Consumption as Transformation**

   Consuming an edible effigy symbolizes the transformation of the spiritual into the physical. By eating these foods, participants internalize the values, blessings, or lessons they represent, completing the ritualistic cycle.

The Gingerbread Golem as a Modern Effigy

The Gingerbread Golem, with its unique combination of sweetness and strength, represents a modern reimagining of the edible effigy.

1. **A Symbol of Protection and Resilience**

   The Gingerbread Golem stands as a protector of holiday traditions and values. Its sturdy, spiced form and decorative features blend the celebratory nature of gingerbread with the protective symbolism of the golem archetype.

2. **Creating Intentional Effigies**

   The act of crafting a Gingerbread Golem can be a meaningful ritual, combining creativity with purpose. Whether baked to guard a home or as a festive centerpiece, the Golem embodies the spirit of resilience and hope.

3. **Blending Sweetness with Seriousness**

   Like traditional edible effigies, the Gingerbread Golem reminds us of the balance between lighthearted celebration and deeper, more solemn themes. Its playful appearance invites joy, while its symbolic role as a sentinel underscores the importance of protecting the values and traditions that matter most.

Conclusion: The Power of Edible Effigies

Edible effigies, from ancient honey cakes to modern gingerbread golems, have long been more than just food. They are symbols of protection, gratitude, and connection, bridging the physical and spiritual worlds. Gingerbread, with its rich history and enduring role in holiday traditions, exemplifies the power of these creations to bring people together, convey profound meanings, and inspire both joy and reflection.

In the Gingerbread Golem, we find the perfect embodiment of the edible effigy: a figure that is sweet yet strong, celebratory yet solemn, playful yet protective. As we continue this exploration of sweet darkness, we uncover not only the traditions that shaped these symbols but also the ways they continue to resonate in our lives today.

Chapter 6: The Duality of Celebration: Light and Dark in Festive Lore

Holidays are often perceived as occasions for unbridled joy, celebration, and togetherness. Yet, beneath the surface of festive lights and cheerful songs lies a darker, more complex tapestry of emotions and traditions. Across cultures and throughout history, holidays have blended themes of joy and dread, light and shadow, to create a deeper, more resonant experience.

This chapter delves into the philosophical underpinnings of this duality, exploring why festive lore so often intertwines the jubilant with the somber and why this balance is essential for creating meaningful celebrations.

The Origins of Duality in Human Experience

The concept of duality—the coexistence of opposing forces—is deeply ingrained in human consciousness. From the earliest myths to modern philosophy, light and dark, life and death, joy and sorrow have been seen as interdependent, each giving meaning to the other.

1. **The Cyclical Nature of Existence**

   Ancient societies viewed time as cyclical, governed by natural rhythms of birth, death, and renewal. The winter season, marked by long nights and barren landscapes, was a time of reflection on mortality and the promise of rebirth. Holidays like Yule, Saturnalia, and later Christmas emerged as celebrations of survival and hope, acknowledging the darkness while invoking the return of light.

2. **Survival Amid Uncertainty**

   For much of human history, winter was a time of scarcity and danger. The festive traditions that arose during this period often contained elements of fear and caution, serving as reminders of the fragility of life. Joy was not taken for granted; it was a hard-earned reprieve from the struggles of survival.

3. **The Emotional Balance of Light and Dark**
   Psychologically, moments of joy are heightened when juxtaposed with moments of darkness. The contrast between light and shadow creates a richer emotional experience, making celebrations more impactful and memorable.

Festive Lore as a Reflection of Duality

Many holiday traditions and myths explicitly incorporate themes of duality, using symbols and narratives to explore the interplay between joy and dread.

1. **The Light of the Hearth vs. the Darkness Outside**
   In winter festivals, the hearth often symbolizes warmth, safety, and community, while the darkness outside represents danger and the unknown. Stories like *A Christmas Carol* by Charles Dickens encapsulate this tension, juxtaposing the comfort of holiday cheer with the harsh realities of greed, loneliness, and mortality.

2. **Figures of Judgment: Reward and Punishment**
   Figures like St. Nicholas and Krampus, or Santa Claus and his "naughty list," embody the duality of holiday lore. These characters reward good behavior while punishing the wicked, reinforcing moral lessons through both joy and fear.

3. **Rituals of Light in the Darkest Days**
   Festivals such as Hanukkah, Diwali, and Yule focus on the symbolism of light overcoming darkness. These celebrations do not ignore the presence of darkness; instead, they use it as a backdrop to emphasize the triumph of hope and resilience.

Why Holidays Must Acknowledge Darkness

Acknowledging the darker aspects of life during celebrations serves several vital purposes, both culturally and psychologically.

1. **Honoring the Complexity of Life**

   Life is not a single-note experience; it is a symphony of contrasting emotions. Celebrations that incorporate elements of darkness recognize this complexity, making them more authentic and emotionally resonant.

2. **Teaching Resilience and Morality**

   Dark themes in festive lore often serve as cautionary tales, teaching resilience, moral behavior, and the importance of community. Legends like the Yule Cat or Perchta remind us of the consequences of selfishness or laziness, while tales of redemption, such as *The Nutcracker,* inspire hope and change.

3. **Creating Catharsis**

   Holidays offer a safe space to confront fears and uncertainties in a controlled, ritualistic way. By acknowledging the darker aspects of life, celebrations allow participants to release pent-up emotions and emerge with a renewed sense of purpose and optimism.

Examples of Light and Dark in Holiday Lore

Many cultural traditions blend joy and dread, illustrating the universality of this duality.

1. **The Wild Hunt and Yule Celebrations**

   The Norse myth of the Wild Hunt, a ghostly procession led by Odin, casts a shadow over Yule celebrations. While the festival celebrates light and warmth, the Wild Hunt reminds revelers of the chaotic, untamed forces that persist during the dark months.

2. **Krampus and St. Nicholas**

   The partnership of Krampus and St. Nicholas exemplifies the interplay of light and dark. While St. Nicholas rewards virtue,

Krampus punishes vice, ensuring that the holiday season balances generosity with discipline.

3. **The Gingerbread Golem**

The Gingerbread Golem, as a modern reinterpretation of festive lore, embodies this duality. Its sweet and whimsical appearance belies its role as a sentinel, standing as both a protector of holiday cheer and a potential enforcer of tradition.

Philosophical Perspectives on Celebration and Duality

1. **Carl Jung: The Shadow and the Psyche**

Swiss psychologist Carl Jung's concept of the shadow—the hidden, darker aspects of the human psyche—provides a framework for understanding why holidays incorporate themes of darkness. By acknowledging and integrating the shadow, individuals and communities achieve greater balance and wholeness.

2. **Nietzsche: Joy in the Face of Tragedy**

Friedrich Nietzsche's philosophy of *amor fati* (love of fate) encourages embracing all aspects of life, including suffering. Holidays that mix joy with sorrow reflect this philosophy, teaching us to find meaning and beauty in the full spectrum of human experience.

3. **Symbolism in Mythology**

Mythologist Joseph Campbell emphasized the importance of symbols in connecting individuals to universal truths. The duality in festive lore—light and dark, joy and dread—acts as a symbolic reminder of life's cyclical nature and humanity's resilience in the face of adversity.

The Role of the Gingerbread Golem in Balancing Duality

The Gingerbread Golem, as a figure in festive lore, encapsulates the duality of celebration.

1. **A Sweet Protector**

   The Golem's sugary exterior and festive origins symbolize light-heartedness, creativity, and joy. Its role as a sentinel, however, adds an element of seriousness, reminding us of the responsibilities that come with celebration.

2. **A Mirror of Human Nature**

   Like the archetypal golem, the Gingerbread Golem reflects the duality within ourselves: the desire to protect and nurture balanced against the capacity for destruction and chaos.

3. **Teaching Balance Through Tradition**

   By blending sweetness with strength, the Gingerbread Golem serves as a metaphor for the balance we seek during the holidays: to enjoy the light while respecting the shadows.

Conclusion: Embracing the Duality of Celebration

The interplay of light and dark in festive lore is not a contradiction but a reflection of life's inherent complexity. Holidays that acknowledge both joy and dread resonate more deeply, offering opportunities for reflection, growth, and connection.

The Gingerbread Golem, as a modern symbol of this duality, invites us to embrace the shadows of the season as much as its light. By doing so, we create celebrations that are not only joyful but also meaningful, rooted in the rich traditions and profound truths that define the human experience.

Chapter 7: Crafting the Golem: The Ritual of Creation

The process of crafting a gingerbread golem is not merely an exercise in baking; it is a profound act of creation imbued with symbolism, intention, and transformation. This chapter explores how the act of baking mirrors ancient rituals of golem-making, serves as a metaphor for creative and spiritual processes, and connects the baker to long-standing traditions of imbuing life and meaning into inanimate forms.

The Golem as a Symbol of Creation

The golem, rooted in Jewish mysticism, is a being formed from raw material—traditionally clay—and brought to life through sacred words or rituals. The Gingerbread Golem, while crafted from dough rather than clay, follows a similar process: an unformed substance is shaped, transformed, and given symbolic life through the act of baking and decoration.

1. **Material Transformation**

   At the heart of golem creation is the transformation of a formless material into a purposeful being. In the case of the Gingerbread Golem, the dough represents potential—soft, malleable, and full of possibility. Through the alchemy of baking, this dough is solidified into something durable and meaningful, echoing the transformative act of creating life.

2. **Intent as the Breath of Life**

   In Jewish mysticism, the golem is animated by the word *emet* (truth) written on its body or spoken into being. Similarly, the Gingerbread Golem is imbued with intention during its creation. The baker's care, creativity, and purpose infuse the final product with symbolic life, turning a simple confection into a sentinel of tradition and spirit.

3. **The Creator-Creation Relationship**

   The process of crafting a Gingerbread Golem reflects the intimate relationship between creator and creation. The baker's hands shape every detail, from the structure of the golem's body to its decorative features, establishing a connection that mirrors the sacred bond in golem mythology.

The Ritual of Baking in Folklore

Baking has long been associated with rituals of creation, transformation, and even magic. The preparation and transformation of ingredients carry deep symbolic meaning in many cultures.

1. **Alchemy in the Kitchen**

   The act of combining simple ingredients—flour, sugar, butter, and spices—and subjecting them to heat mirrors the alchemical process of turning base materials into gold. In baking, the transformation of dough into a solid, fragrant creation symbolizes the power of human ingenuity to bring order and beauty to the natural world.

2. **Baking as a Communal Act**

   Historically, baking has been a communal activity, bringing people together to create sustenance and celebrate rituals. Crafting gingerbread golems, whether as a family or community project, echoes the collective effort involved in ancient ceremonies of creation.

3. **Food as Sacred Offering**

   Many cultures view baking as a sacred act, with the final product serving as an offering to deities, spirits, or the community. Gingerbread figures, with their intricate designs and festive associations, retain this sense of sacred purpose, acting as edible effigies that honor tradition and invite protection.

Steps in Crafting a Gingerbread Golem

The ritual of crafting a Gingerbread Golem involves multiple steps, each rich with symbolic meaning.

1. **Preparing the Ingredients**

   The selection and preparation of ingredients symbolize the gathering of raw materials. Spices like ginger and cinnamon carry historical and spiritual significance, representing warmth, protection, and vitality.

2. **Kneading the Dough**

   Kneading the dough transforms disparate ingredients into a cohesive whole, symbolizing unity and the molding of raw potential into a purposeful form. This step mirrors the shaping of clay in traditional golem-making, where the creator imbues their material with intention.

3. **Shaping the Golem**

   Shaping the dough into the form of a golem is an act of imagination and intention. Every detail, from its size to its decorations, carries meaning, reflecting the creator's vision and purpose.

4. **Baking as Transformation**

   The act of baking represents the moment of transformation, where the formless becomes formed, and potential is realized. The heat of the oven serves as a metaphor for the trials and challenges that solidify one's identity and purpose.

5. **Decorating the Golem**

   Decorating the Gingerbread Golem brings it to life, giving it personality and symbolic features. Buttons, icing, and patterns can be imbued with meaning, turning the golem into a unique reflection of its creator's intention.

6. **Naming and Purpose**

   Just as the traditional golem is given life through the inscription of a name or sacred word, the Gingerbread Golem can be personalized with a name or role. Whether it serves as a festive guardian, a symbol of family unity, or a playful centerpiece, its purpose completes the ritual of creation.

The Symbolism of Heat and Transformation

The oven, a central element in baking, holds profound symbolic meaning in the creation process.

1. **The Womb of Creation**

   The oven represents a sacred space where transformation occurs, akin to a womb. The dough, placed into this space, undergoes a metamorphosis, emerging as something new and complete.

2. **Trials and Tempering**

   The heat of the oven symbolizes the challenges and trials that strengthen and refine the golem. This parallels the mythological idea of heroes or creations being tested by fire to prove their worth.

3. **The Moment of Emergence**

   The act of removing the Gingerbread Golem from the oven mirrors the moment of birth or creation, where the intangible (intention, imagination) becomes tangible and real.

Baking as a Metaphor for Personal Transformation

The ritual of baking, particularly the creation of a Gingerbread Golem, can also be seen as a metaphor for personal growth and transformation.

1. **Gathering the Ingredients of Life**

   Just as baking requires the right combination of ingredients, personal transformation involves gathering the right experiences, skills, and values.

2. **Kneading Through Challenges**

   The process of kneading reflects the effort and perseverance needed to shape one's identity. The pressure and movement required to form the dough mirror the struggles that mold character and resilience.

3. **Embracing Heat as Growth**

   The heat of the oven represents the challenges and difficulties that temper us, turning raw potential into strength and purpose.

4. **Emerging as a Complete Creation**

   The final product—a beautifully crafted Gingerbread Golem—symbolizes the culmination of effort, intention, and transformation, serving as a reminder of the power of creation in all its forms.

The Gingerbread Golem's Role in Tradition

As a modern interpretation of the golem myth, the Gingerbread Golem embodies the timeless themes of creation and transformation.

1. **A Sentinel of Celebration**
   The Gingerbread Golem serves as a protector of holiday traditions, its sweet form and festive decorations symbolizing the resilience of joy and community.
2. **A Reflection of the Creator**
   Each Gingerbread Golem is a unique creation, reflecting the imagination, care, and purpose of its maker. This individuality reinforces the idea that creation is an act of self-expression.
3. **A Bridge Between Past and Present**
   By crafting a Gingerbread Golem, modern bakers connect with ancient traditions of edible effigies and ritualistic creation, blending the old with the new in a celebration of continuity and innovation.

Conclusion: The Sacred Act of Creation

Crafting a Gingerbread Golem is more than a holiday tradition; it is a sacred act of creation that mirrors the transformative power of life itself. Through the careful selection of ingredients, the ritualistic process of baking, and the final act of decoration, the Gingerbread Golem becomes a symbol of resilience, intention, and celebration.

As a metaphor for creation and transformation, the Gingerbread Golem invites us to reflect on our own processes of growth and change. By embracing the ritual of baking, we not only honor ancient traditions but also participate in the timeless act of turning potential into purpose, one sweet creation at a time.

Chapter 8: The Gingerbread Man: From Folk Tale to Folk Terror

The story of the Gingerbread Man is a tale of whimsy that has delighted children for generations. At its surface, it's a simple narrative of a cookie that springs to life, boldly declares its independence, and meets its inevitable fate. But beneath the sugary coating lies a narrative with darker undertones—one that speaks to themes of hubris, pursuit, and the consequences of unchecked ambition.

This chapter explores the origins of the Gingerbread Man story, its evolution from lighthearted folk tale to a more sinister interpretation, and its role as a cautionary tale that mirrors humanity's struggles with creation, autonomy, and mortality.

The Origins of the Gingerbread Man Story

The earliest recorded version of the Gingerbread Man tale appeared in the United States in 1875 in *St. Nicholas Magazine*. The story, penned by an anonymous author, begins in a familiar fashion: a lonely woman bakes a gingerbread figure, only for it to spring to life and escape her grasp.

1. **A Product of Oral Tradition**

   While the 1875 publication marked the Gingerbread Man's first appearance in print, the story's roots likely extend back to older European oral traditions. Folk tales about anthropomorphic food items, magical creations, and mischievous figures were common in medieval storytelling. These tales often served as entertainment but also carried moral or cautionary messages.

2. **Early Themes in the Tale**

   The Gingerbread Man's story aligns with broader folkloric motifs of creation and pursuit. Its central themes—hubris, defiance, and inevitable downfall—reflect universal struggles with authority, independence, and the consequences of one's actions.

3. **Symbolism of the Gingerbread Man's Creation**

   The Gingerbread Man, as a baked creation brought to life, shares similarities with other folkloric constructs like the golem or Frankenstein's monster. These figures symbolize humanity's desire to create and control life, as well as the potential dangers of doing so without foresight or restraint.

The Evolution of the Tale

Over time, the Gingerbread Man's story evolved, taking on different forms and interpretations that reflected cultural anxieties and shifting societal values.

1. **The Escapist Narrative**

   In its earliest versions, the Gingerbread Man is a figure of defiance and escape. His repeated refrain, "Run, run, as fast as you can! You can't catch me; I'm the Gingerbread Man!" embodies a spirit of rebellion and independence. Yet, his hubris ultimately leads to his downfall, teaching a lesson about the perils of overconfidence.

2. **Cautionary Elements**

   The Gingerbread Man's story carries a clear moral: actions have consequences, and recklessness leads to ruin. The character's refusal to heed warnings or respect boundaries results in his demise, a fate that underscores the importance of humility and caution.

3. **Modern Retellings and Variations**

   In modern adaptations, the tale has been reimagined in ways that highlight different aspects of the story. Some versions emphasize the Gingerbread Man's cleverness and wit, while others focus on his arrogance and foolishness. These variations reflect the adaptability of folklore, which evolves to suit the values and concerns of its audience.

Darker Undertones of the Gingerbread Man

While often viewed as a lighthearted children's story, the Gingerbread Man tale contains elements that lend themselves to darker interpretations.

1. **The Pursuit and the Predator**

   The Gingerbread Man's escape and eventual capture mirror themes of pursuit and predation found in many cautionary tales. Each character in the story—be it the old woman, the cow, or the fox—represents a different kind of threat, highlighting the dangers that lurk in the world.

2. **The Deceptive Fox**

   The fox, who ultimately tricks and devours the Gingerbread Man, symbolizes cunning and treachery. This character's role introduces an element of betrayal, showing that the greatest danger often comes from those who feign assistance or friendship.

3. **A Metaphor for Mortality**

   The Gingerbread Man's journey, from creation to escape to destruction, can be interpreted as a metaphor for the human experience. His brief life, filled with bold defiance and inevitable downfall, mirrors humanity's struggle with the fleeting nature of existence.

Connections to Other Folk Horror Narratives

The Gingerbread Man's tale shares thematic elements with other folk horror traditions, which often blend whimsy with unsettling or macabre undertones.

1. **The Golem Connection**

   Like the Gingerbread Man, the golem is a creation that springs to life and ultimately disrupts the balance of its creator's world. Both figures raise questions about the responsibilities of creation and the limits of human control.

2. **Hansel and Gretel**

   The Gingerbread Man's connection to food-based folklore is echoed in tales like *Hansel and Gretel*, where a house made of candy lures children to their doom. These stories use food as a symbol of temptation and danger, reinforcing the idea that indulgence often comes at a cost.

3. **The Animistic Food Trope**

   Stories of food coming to life, such as enchanted cakes or bread effigies, often carry themes of magic and rebellion. These narratives blur the line between the mundane and the mystical, inviting both delight and unease.

The Gingerbread Man as Folk Terror

In recent years, the Gingerbread Man has taken on a new life in horror and dark fantasy genres, where his story has been reimagined with terrifying twists.

1. **Revenge of the Gingerbread Man**

    Modern horror adaptations often depict the Gingerbread Man as a vengeful figure, seeking retribution against those who created or wronged him. These narratives flip the original story, turning the pursued into the pursuer.

2. **The Gingerbread Golem**

    The Gingerbread Golem, as a variation of the Gingerbread Man, transforms the whimsical figure into a powerful sentinel. This reinterpretation emphasizes the darker potential of a creation that refuses to be controlled.

3. **Horror and Humor**

    The Gingerbread Man's transformation into a figure of terror often blends horror with humor, creating a subversive take on the original tale. Films like *The Gingerdead Man* capitalize on this duality, using the incongruity of a killer cookie to evoke both laughter and fear.

The Lessons of the Gingerbread Man

Despite its darker undertones, the story of the Gingerbread Man remains a timeless tale with valuable lessons.

1. **The Danger of Hubris**

   The Gingerbread Man's overconfidence and refusal to heed warnings serve as a cautionary tale about the consequences of arrogance and recklessness.

2. **The Complexity of Freedom**

   While the Gingerbread Man's escape symbolizes a desire for freedom, his fate highlights the challenges and dangers that come with independence.

3. **The Power of Adaptation**

   The enduring appeal of the Gingerbread Man lies in his adaptability. Whether as a whimsical figure or a symbol of terror, his story continues to resonate because it reflects universal truths about creation, autonomy, and the human condition.

Conclusion: From Sweet Treat to Shadowy Symbol

The Gingerbread Man's journey from folk tale to folk terror is a testament to the power of storytelling. What began as a simple narrative about a mischievous cookie has evolved into a complex, multifaceted tale that explores themes of creation, defiance, and mortality.

As we continue to reimagine the Gingerbread Man in contexts like the Gingerbread Golem, we uncover new layers of meaning in his story. Whether sweet or sinister, his tale remains a rich and enduring part of our cultural imagination, inviting us to confront the light and dark within ourselves.

Chapter 9: Sweetness and Strength: The Paradox of the Gingerbread Golem

The Gingerbread Golem is a curious fusion of whimsy and menace, its sweet exterior concealing an inner core of strength and potential danger. This paradox—an edible creation meant to evoke joy yet imbued with the archetypal power of a golem—highlights the complex interplay of light and dark that defines both its character and its cultural significance.

In this chapter, we explore the symbolic nature of the Gingerbread Golem, delving into how its delicate sweetness contrasts with its latent power and potential for destruction. Through a philosophical and folkloric lens, we examine the broader implications of this paradox and what it reveals about humanity's relationship with creation, control, and duality.

The Sweet Exterior: A Symbol of Innocence and Joy

The Gingerbread Golem's outward appearance, crafted from dough and decorated with colorful icing and candies, is a visual delight. Its sugary aesthetic evokes childhood nostalgia, holiday cheer, and communal celebration.

1. **A Festive Tradition**

   The creation of gingerbread figures is deeply rooted in holiday traditions. From gingerbread men to elaborately designed gingerbread houses, these treats are synonymous with warmth, family, and festivity. The Gingerbread Golem, with its playful appearance, builds on this tradition, embodying the spirit of joy and creativity.

2. **Edible Artistry**

   The act of decorating a Gingerbread Golem is an exercise in artistic expression. The use of icing, candy, and intricate patterns transforms the golem into a work of edible art, its delicate details underscoring its fragile nature.

3. **A Surface of Innocence**

   The sweet exterior of the Gingerbread Golem suggests innocence and harmlessness. This outward simplicity, however, is deceptive—a deliberate contrast to the deeper, more complex nature that lies within.

The Inner Strength: The Golem's Archetypal Power

Beneath its sugary surface, the Gingerbread Golem carries the symbolic weight of the golem archetype—a figure of immense strength, unquestioning loyalty, and latent power.

1. **A Construct of Purpose**

   Like traditional golems fashioned from clay or stone, the Gingerbread Golem is a creation of intent. Its strength and abilities derive not from its materials but from the purpose and intention imbued in it by its creator.

2. **Symbolic Strength**

   The Gingerbread Golem's strength is not physical in the conventional sense; rather, it represents resilience and protection. As a festive sentinel, it guards against the stresses and disruptions of the holiday season, embodying the ideals of perseverance and stability.

3. **Potential for Power and Destruction**

   As with all golems, the Gingerbread Golem's strength carries a dual potential: it can be a force for protection or destruction. While its purpose is to safeguard holiday traditions, its latent power raises questions about what might happen if that power were misused or unleashed.

The Paradox of Sweetness and Strength

The juxtaposition of the Gingerbread Golem's sugary exterior and its symbolic strength creates a powerful paradox, one that mirrors broader themes in folklore, mythology, and human experience.

1. **Fragility and Fortitude**

   The Gingerbread Golem is both fragile and formidable. Its edible construction makes it susceptible to breaking, yet its symbolic role as a protector imbues it with an unyielding strength. This duality reflects the human condition, where vulnerability and resilience coexist.

2. **Whimsy and Warning**

   The playful appearance of the Gingerbread Golem belies its deeper significance as a cautionary figure. It reminds us that even the sweetest creations can possess a hidden strength, and that joy and danger often exist side by side.

3. **Control and Chaos**

   Like the traditional golem, the Gingerbread Golem is a creation of human intent, bound to its creator's will. Yet its potential for power suggests the possibility of chaos, echoing the age-old cautionary tale of creation exceeding control.

Parallels in Folklore and Mythology

The paradox of the Gingerbread Golem is not unique; similar themes appear throughout folklore and mythology, where seemingly harmless or sweet figures conceal great power.

1. **The Trojan Horse**
   The Trojan Horse, a seemingly benign gift that concealed a deadly threat, shares thematic similarities with the Gingerbread Golem. Both highlight the danger of underestimating appearances and the potential for hidden power to upend expectations.

2. **Fairy Tale Transformations**
   Many fairy tales feature characters or objects that appear innocent but possess transformative power. From Cinderella's pumpkin carriage to Sleeping Beauty's spinning wheel, these stories explore the tension between surface appearances and deeper truths.

3. **The Trickster Archetype**
   Figures like Loki in Norse mythology or Anansi in African folklore embody the paradox of charm and danger. Like the Gingerbread Golem, they remind us that sweetness and strength often go hand in hand, challenging our assumptions and inviting deeper reflection.

The Philosophical Implications of the Paradox

The Gingerbread Golem's paradox of sweetness and strength raises profound philosophical questions about creation, power, and the human condition.

1. **What Does It Mean to Create?**

   The act of crafting a Gingerbread Golem invites reflection on the responsibilities of creation. How do we balance the desire to create something beautiful and joyful with the potential for that creation to wield power or cause harm?

2. **The Nature of Strength**

   The Gingerbread Golem challenges traditional notions of strength, suggesting that true power lies not in physical might but in purpose, intention, and resilience.

3. **The Tension Between Control and Autonomy**

   As a creation bound to its maker's will, the Gingerbread Golem embodies the tension between control and autonomy. This dynamic reflects broader questions about agency, free will, and the ethical limits of creation.

The Gingerbread Golem as a Modern Archetype

The Gingerbread Golem's unique blend of sweetness and strength makes it a compelling modern archetype, one that resonates with contemporary concerns and values.

1. **A Symbol of Holiday Resilience**

   As a festive figure, the Gingerbread Golem represents the resilience and strength needed to navigate the challenges of the holiday season. Its presence offers both comfort and inspiration, reminding us that even in times of stress, sweetness and joy can prevail.

2. **A Reflection of Duality**

   The Gingerbread Golem embodies the duality of human nature—the ability to be both gentle and strong, playful and serious, sweet and powerful. This duality makes it a relatable and enduring symbol.

3. **An Invitation to Reflection**

   By confronting us with its paradoxical nature, the Gingerbread Golem invites deeper reflection on the complexities of creation, strength, and the balance between light and dark.

Conclusion: The Power of Paradox

The Gingerbread Golem's paradox of sweetness and strength is a powerful metaphor for the complexities of life and creation. Its sugary exterior and latent power remind us that appearances can be deceiving, and that even the most fragile creations can possess great strength.

As we continue to explore the role of the Gingerbread Golem in festive lore, we uncover not only its symbolic significance but also the deeper truths it reveals about resilience, duality, and the enduring power of creation. Through this paradoxical figure, we are reminded that joy and strength, light and shadow, sweetness and power are not opposites but essential facets of the same whole.

Chapter 10: Fear in the Frost: Winter's Psychological Shadows

Winter, with its long nights, biting cold, and stark landscapes, has always held a unique power over the human psyche. For centuries, the season has inspired tales of mystery, fear, and the supernatural. The psychological shadows of winter—manifested in folkloric monsters like Krampus, the Yule Cat, and now the Gingerbread Golem—speak to our collective anxieties and survival instincts.

This chapter explores why cold, dark winters foster these chilling tales, how they reflect the human experience of the season, and why monsters like the Gingerbread Golem emerge as symbolic figures of both dread and resilience.

The Psychological Impact of Winter

Winter is a season of extremes, marked by harsh environmental conditions and significant psychological challenges.

1. **The Isolation of Darkness**

   The extended darkness of winter can evoke feelings of isolation and vulnerability. Before the advent of modern lighting and heating, the absence of sunlight created an almost primal fear of the unknown, fueling imaginations with visions of lurking dangers.

2. **Survival Anxiety**

   In agrarian and pre-industrial societies, winter was a time of scarcity. Food stores dwindled, and the threat of illness and death loomed large. This sense of existential fragility often found expression in folklore, where monsters symbolized the fears of starvation, illness, and community breakdown.

3. **Seasonal Affective Disorder (SAD)**

   Modern psychology recognizes the effects of prolonged darkness on mental health. Seasonal affective disorder, characterized by depression and lethargy during the winter months, mirrors the emotional shadows that permeate winter folklore.

Why Monsters Emerge in Winter Folklore

The monsters of winter folklore are not mere flights of fancy; they are reflections of deeply rooted fears and survival instincts.

1. **Embodiments of the Unknown**

   Winter monsters often personify the unknown dangers of the season. From wolves howling in the night to the unseen forces of a blizzard, these creatures give form to the intangible threats of winter.

2. **Warnings and Lessons**

   Tales of winter monsters often carry moral or practical lessons. Krampus punishes misbehaving children, while the Yule Cat targets those who fail to prepare properly for the season. These stories reinforced social norms and survival behaviors, ensuring that communities remained vigilant and cooperative during the harsh months.

3. **Catharsis Through Fear**

   Fear, when channeled through storytelling, becomes a tool for catharsis. Tales of winter monsters allow communities to confront and process their anxieties in a controlled and symbolic way, making the season's challenges more manageable.

The Gingerbread Golem: A New Winter Monster

The Gingerbread Golem, though a modern invention, draws upon the same psychological and folkloric traditions as older winter monsters.

1. **A Symbol of Overindulgence**

   The Gingerbread Golem reflects the tension between the abundance of holiday celebrations and the scarcity of winter. Its origins as a festive treat gone awry remind us of the dangers of excess and the importance of balance during the season.

2. **A Protector Turned Punisher**

   Like many winter monsters, the Gingerbread Golem straddles the line between guardian and threat. Its role as a sentinel of holiday traditions can easily shift into one of vengeance if those traditions are neglected or disrespected.

3. **The Sweet Mask of Danger**

   The Gingerbread Golem's sugary appearance belies its potential for menace, echoing the deceptive charm of other folkloric figures like the Pied Piper or Hansel and Gretel's witch. This duality makes it a compelling addition to the pantheon of winter monsters.

Monsters as Mirrors of Human Fears

Winter monsters often reveal more about human nature and societal fears than they do about the external world.

1. **The Fear of Isolation**

   Monsters like the Gingerbread Golem emerge in tales where the community has failed to uphold its values, reflecting the fear of isolation and disconnection. Winter, with its isolating conditions, amplifies this anxiety.

2. **The Consequences of Neglect**

   Many winter monsters, including the Gingerbread Golem, punish those who neglect their duties or responsibilities. These tales reinforce the importance of preparation, generosity, and adherence to tradition during challenging times.

3. **The Shadow of Excess**

   Holiday monsters often emerge as cautionary figures against overindulgence or selfishness. The Gingerbread Golem's sweet exterior serves as a reminder that unchecked indulgence can lead to unexpected consequences.

The Role of Environment in Shaping Winter Lore

The physical and environmental challenges of winter play a significant role in the development of its folklore.

1. **The Harshness of the Landscape**

   Snow-covered fields, barren trees, and frozen rivers create a stark and otherworldly backdrop for winter tales. This desolate environment fosters a sense of unease and provides the perfect stage for supernatural stories.

2. **The Threat of Predators**

   In earlier times, winter brought humans into closer contact with natural predators, such as wolves and bears, whose presence is reflected in the fearsome characteristics of many winter monsters.

3. **The Silence of Snow**

   The muffling effect of snow creates an eerie silence that amplifies feelings of isolation and vulnerability. This sensory experience has inspired tales of monsters that move unseen or strike without warning, like the spectral figures of the Wild Hunt.

The Symbolism of Frost and Cold

Cold itself is often personified in winter folklore, taking on a dual role as both destroyer and preserver.

1. **Frost as a Life Force**

   While frost can kill crops and chill the body, it also preserves food and protects the land by signaling a period of rest before spring. This duality mirrors the Gingerbread Golem's role as both protector and potential punisher.

2. **The Inescapability of Winter**

   Cold is relentless, unavoidable, and impartial, much like the judgment of winter monsters. The Gingerbread Golem, as a creation bound to the season, embodies this inescapable force, serving as a reminder of nature's power.

Why We Need Winter Monsters

Monsters like the Gingerbread Golem serve an essential purpose in human storytelling, particularly during winter.

1. **Exploring Duality**

   Winter monsters embody the dual nature of the season—its beauty and brutality, its capacity for both generosity and scarcity. They invite us to reflect on these contrasts and find meaning in them.

2. **Reinforcing Community Bonds**

   By confronting shared fears through storytelling, winter monsters strengthen community ties. The lessons they impart—about preparation, cooperation, and respect for tradition—ensure that communities remain united in the face of hardship.

3. **Celebrating Resilience**

   Ultimately, tales of winter monsters celebrate humanity's ability to endure and overcome. By acknowledging the shadows of the season, we gain a deeper appreciation for the light and warmth that define our celebrations.

Conclusion: The Shadows That Shape Us

The psychological shadows of winter, embodied in monsters like the Gingerbread Golem, reflect our deepest fears and greatest strengths. These tales remind us that while the season may bring challenges, it also offers opportunities for growth, reflection, and renewal.

As a modern addition to this rich tradition, the Gingerbread Golem invites us to embrace both the sweetness and the strength of the season, finding meaning not only in the light but also in the frost-covered shadows that shape our collective imagination.

Chapter 11: The Golem and the Hearth: Protecting the Home

The hearth has long been a symbol of safety, warmth, and community, particularly during the harshness of winter. In folklore and tradition, the hearth serves as the center of the home, a place where food is prepared, stories are shared, and the chill of the outside world is kept at bay. Similarly, the Gingerbread Golem, as a modern interpretation of the golem archetype, emerges as a guardian figure tied to the hearth, charged with protecting the home and family during the season of cold and darkness.

This chapter delves into the historical and symbolic connections between the hearth and protective figures, examines how the Gingerbread Golem fulfills the role of a home sentinel, and explores the cultural and psychological significance of home protection during winter.

The Hearth as the Heart of the Home

1. **The Historical Significance of the Hearth**

   In pre-industrial societies, the hearth was the central feature of a household. It provided heat for warmth, light for visibility, and fire for cooking. During winter, when survival depended on communal efforts and careful resource management, the hearth symbolized life itself.

2. **The Hearth in Myth and Folklore**

   Across cultures, the hearth was often associated with deities or spirits tasked with protecting the home. In Roman mythology, Vesta, the goddess of the hearth, was worshiped as the guardian of domestic life. Similarly, in Slavic traditions, the *domovoi*—a house spirit—was believed to inhabit the hearth, safeguarding the household from harm.

3. **The Hearth as a Symbol of Unity**

   The hearth was also a gathering place, where families and communities came together to share meals, stories, and rituals. This unity reinforced the idea of the home as a sanctuary, a space that needed to be protected from external threats.

The Golem as a Protector of the Home

1. **The Role of the Golem in Folklore**

   Traditional golems, created from clay and brought to life through mystical means, were often tasked with protecting specific places or people. In Jewish folklore, the golem guarded synagogues and communities from harm, standing as a silent sentinel against external threats.

2. **The Gingerbread Golem's Protective Nature**

   As a confectionery reinterpretation of this archetype, the Gingerbread Golem assumes the role of a household protector. Its sweet, festive appearance aligns it with the warmth and joy of the hearth, while its symbolic strength connects it to the enduring themes of safety and resilience.

3. **A Sentinel for the Season**

   The Gingerbread Golem is particularly suited to its role as a winter guardian. During the coldest and darkest months of the year, the home becomes a sanctuary, and the Gingerbread Golem stands as a symbolic protector of the family's well-being and the traditions that sustain them.

The Gingerbread Golem in the Context of Winter Protection

1. **Guarding Against the Physical Threats of Winter**
   In earlier times, winter brought tangible dangers such as frostbite, illness, and food scarcity. Folklore often personified these threats in the form of malevolent spirits or creatures. The Gingerbread Golem, while not a literal protector, symbolizes the community's efforts to prepare for and withstand these challenges.

2. **Ward Against Malevolent Forces**
   Many winter traditions include rituals to protect the home from supernatural forces believed to be more active during the season. Gingerbread effigies, shaped as festive guardians, echo these protective practices. The Gingerbread Golem's imposing yet cheerful form can be seen as a modern-day talisman against the shadows of winter.

3. **Preserving the Holiday Spirit**
   The Gingerbread Golem's role extends beyond physical protection to the safeguarding of intangible elements like joy, unity, and tradition. By embodying the values of the season, it serves as a reminder to cherish and uphold the bonds that make the home a haven.

The Act of Creation as a Protective Ritual

1. **Crafting the Gingerbread Golem as a Family Activity**
   The process of baking and decorating a Gingerbread Golem can be seen as a ritualistic act that brings families together. The shared effort of creating a guardian figure reinforces familial bonds and instills a sense of collective purpose.

2. **Infusing the Golem with Intent**
   Just as traditional golems were animated through sacred words and rituals, the Gingerbread Golem is imbued with meaning and intent through the act of its creation. The care and creativity that go into crafting the golem symbolize the family's commitment to protecting their home and traditions.

3. **Placing the Golem as a Symbol of Protection**
   Once completed, the Gingerbread Golem can be placed in a prominent location within the home, such as near the hearth or as a centerpiece. Its presence serves as both a festive decoration and a symbolic guardian, reminding the family of the values and efforts that sustain them through the winter.

The Psychological Need for Home Protection

1. **The Home as a Sanctuary**
   The concept of home carries profound psychological significance. It is a place of safety and comfort, where individuals can retreat from the stresses and uncertainties of the outside world. The Gingerbread Golem, as a guardian figure, represents the desire to maintain this sanctuary against both physical and emotional threats.

2. **Winter's Amplification of Fear and Vulnerability**
   The long nights and cold temperatures of winter heighten feelings of vulnerability, making the need for protective symbols more pronounced. The Gingerbread Golem provides a sense of reassurance, embodying the resilience and warmth needed to endure the season.

3. **Rituals as a Source of Stability**
   Engaging in protective rituals, such as creating and placing a Gingerbread Golem, helps to alleviate anxiety and foster a sense of control. These acts connect individuals to a larger tradition, offering comfort and continuity in the face of uncertainty.

The Hearth, the Golem, and Modern Traditions

1. **Reviving the Role of the Hearth**
   In contemporary life, the hearth has largely been replaced by central heating and electric stoves. However, the symbolic role of the hearth as the heart of the home endures. The Gingerbread Golem, as a guardian figure tied to the hearth, helps to revive this connection, reminding families of the warmth and unity that define the holiday season.

2. **The Golem in a Digital Age**
   As modern life becomes increasingly digital and fragmented, traditions like baking a Gingerbread Golem provide a tactile, shared experience that grounds individuals in the physical and the present.

3. **A Modern Myth for the Home**
   The Gingerbread Golem represents a new mythological figure for the winter season, one that blends ancient themes of protection with the festive charm of holiday traditions. Its role as a guardian of the home speaks to timeless human needs while offering a fresh and imaginative take on seasonal lore.

Conclusion: The Gingerbread Golem and the Protected Hearth

The Gingerbread Golem, with its roots in the golem archetype and its ties to the hearth, stands as a powerful symbol of home protection. In the cold and darkness of winter, it embodies the resilience, unity, and warmth that make the home a sanctuary.

By crafting and honoring the Gingerbread Golem, families not only engage in a festive tradition but also affirm their commitment to preserving the values and connections that sustain them through life's challenges. In this way, the Gingerbread Golem becomes more than a sweet treat or a decorative figure—it becomes a sentinel of the hearth and a guardian of the heart.

Chapter 12: Sweet Darkness: The Allure of the Macabre in Festive Tales

The holiday season is a time of celebration, warmth, and joy, but it also holds a curious space for darkness. From ghostly tales told by the fire to cautionary folklore featuring shadowy figures like Krampus and the Yule Cat, the macabre has long been woven into festive traditions. This paradox—mixing lighthearted festivity with chilling themes—has captivated generations and remains an essential part of our seasonal storytelling.

In this chapter, we explore why dark themes hold such an allure during the holidays, how they enrich traditions by adding depth and complexity, and how figures like the Gingerbread Golem embody this duality of sweetness and shadow.

The Origins of Darkness in Festive Traditions

The intertwining of dark themes with festive tales can be traced back to the ancient roots of winter celebrations.

1. **The Winter Solstice and the Shadows of the Season**
   Ancient winter solstice festivals, such as Yule and Saturnalia, were held during the darkest days of the year. These celebrations marked the return of the sun but also acknowledged the long nights, cold weather, and dangers of winter. The darkness was not merely a backdrop but a central theme, reflecting the precarious balance between survival and loss.

2. **A Time of Reflection and Mortality**
   Winter's starkness often prompted reflections on mortality,

scarcity, and the cyclical nature of life. Storytelling during this time frequently included somber or cautionary tales, which served both as entertainment and as a way to process collective fears.

3. **Folklore as a Survival Mechanism**
   Many festive tales were rooted in practical concerns. Stories of malevolent creatures like the Yule Cat or Perchta, the belly-slitting witch, were used to encourage preparation and hard work during winter. These narratives, while macabre, reinforced the values and behaviors necessary for survival.

The Psychological Appeal of the Macabre

Dark themes during the holidays may seem counterintuitive, but they serve important psychological and emotional purposes.

1. **Contrast Heightens Joy**
   The juxtaposition of darkness with light makes the joy of the season more profound. Stories with macabre elements create an emotional balance, allowing us to appreciate the warmth and safety of the holidays by confronting their opposite.

2. **Catharsis Through Fear**
   Tales of monsters, spirits, and other shadowy figures allow us to explore and release our fears in a controlled environment. This catharsis is particularly potent during winter, when the natural world can feel harsh and unforgiving.

3. **Connection to the Unseen**
   Dark festive tales often explore themes of the supernatural, bridging the gap between the mundane and the mystical. These stories invite us to engage with the unknown and embrace the mysteries that define human experience.

Dark Figures in Festive Tales

The macabre in holiday lore often takes the form of shadowy figures who embody the season's duality.

1. **Krampus: The Dark Enforcer**

   Krampus, the horned companion of St. Nicholas, is one of the most iconic examples of festive darkness. While St. Nicholas rewards good behavior, Krampus punishes the wicked, ensuring balance and discipline. His fearsome appearance and punitive actions create a stark contrast to the joy of the season, making his inclusion in festive traditions both thrilling and meaningful.

2. **The Yule Cat: A Creature of Fear and Motivation**

   The Icelandic Yule Cat (*Jólakötturinn*) prowls the countryside, devouring those who fail to receive new clothing for Christmas. This tale, while terrifying, served a practical purpose: encouraging generosity and preparation in a harsh winter climate.

3. **Ghost Stories by the Fire**

   In Victorian England, ghost stories were a popular holiday pastime. Charles Dickens' *A Christmas Carol* remains one of the most enduring examples, blending spectral hauntings with themes of redemption and the spirit of giving.

4. **The Gingerbread Golem: Sweet Yet Sinister**

   The Gingerbread Golem, with its sugary exterior and symbolic strength, exemplifies the blend of sweetness and darkness. It serves as both a festive figure and a cautionary presence, reminding us of the consequences of neglecting tradition or overindulging in holiday excess.

The Role of Dark Tales in Enriching Traditions

Dark festive tales do more than entertain—they add depth and complexity to our traditions.

1. **Reinforcing Moral Lessons**

   Many macabre holiday tales serve as cautionary stories, teaching important lessons about generosity, preparation, and community. The fear they evoke ensures that these lessons are remembered and passed down through generations.

2. **Celebrating Resilience**

   By confronting darkness in stories, we celebrate our ability to endure and overcome challenges. The inclusion of shadowy themes in holiday lore reminds us of our resilience and the importance of hope.

3. **Bridging the Past and Present**

   Dark festive tales connect us to the ancient roots of holiday traditions, preserving their original meanings while adapting them to contemporary contexts. Figures like the Gingerbread Golem honor these connections by blending timeless themes with modern creativity.

The Gingerbread Golem: A Modern Example of Sweet Darkness

1. **A Guardian and a Warning**
   The Gingerbread Golem, as a festive sentinel, embodies the duality of light and dark. Its role as a protector of holiday traditions is juxtaposed with its potential for menace, reflecting the tension between joy and discipline in festive lore.

2. **A Symbol of Seasonal Balance**
   Like Krampus or the Yule Cat, the Gingerbread Golem reminds us of the importance of balance during the holidays. Its sweet exterior represents the lightheartedness of the season, while its golem-like strength underscores the seriousness of its purpose.

3. **An Invitation to Reflection**
   The Gingerbread Golem's paradoxical nature invites us to reflect on the complexities of the season. It challenges us to embrace both the sweetness and the shadows of the holidays, finding meaning in their interplay.

Why We Crave Sweet Darkness

The allure of dark festive tales lies in their ability to deepen our connection to the season and to ourselves.

1. **They Acknowledge Life's Complexity**

   The holidays are not purely joyful; they are also a time of reflection, nostalgia, and even sorrow. Dark tales honor these emotions, allowing us to celebrate in a way that feels authentic and complete.

2. **They Create Memorable Stories**

   Stories that blend sweetness and darkness leave a lasting impression. The contrasts they present make them more engaging and impactful, ensuring their place in cultural memory.

3. **They Offer a Safe Exploration of Fear**

   By engaging with dark themes in a festive context, we can explore our fears in a safe and controlled way. This exploration helps us to process these emotions and emerge with a renewed sense of hope and strength.

Conclusion: Sweet Darkness and the Spirit of the Season

The macabre elements of festive tales, far from detracting from the joy of the holidays, enrich them by adding depth, contrast, and meaning. Figures like Krampus, the Yule Cat, and the Gingerbread Golem remind us that the holidays are not just about light and laughter—they are also a time to confront and embrace the shadows that make the light shine brighter.

As we continue to tell and create stories that blend sweetness and darkness, we honor the full spectrum of human experience, celebrating not only the warmth of the hearth but also the mysteries that linger in the frost-covered shadows. Through this balance, we find a richer, more resonant way to connect with the season and with each other.

Chapter 13: Symbolism of Spices: The Alchemical Roots of Gingerbread

Gingerbread, with its warm, aromatic blend of spices, is more than just a festive treat; it is a culinary expression of history, mysticism, and alchemy. The spices used in gingerbread—ginger, cinnamon, nutmeg, clove, and others—carry profound symbolic meanings, reflecting centuries of cultural, medicinal, and spiritual significance. From their origins in ancient trade routes to their role in medieval alchemy, these spices imbue gingerbread with a richness that transcends taste.

This chapter explores the mystical and historical roots of the spices in gingerbread, examining their symbolic meanings, their alchemical associations, and the ways in which they elevate gingerbread into a creation that bridges the physical and spiritual realms.

The Historical Significance of Spices

1. **The Spice Trade and Global Connection**
   The spices found in gingerbread were once among the most coveted commodities in the world. Traded along ancient routes like the Silk Road, spices such as ginger, cinnamon, and nutmeg were prized not only for their flavor but also for their perceived medicinal and mystical properties.
   - **Ginger** originated in Southeast Asia and was valued for its warming properties and ability to treat ailments.
   - **Cinnamon**, derived from the bark of Cinnamomum trees, was considered a gift worthy of gods and kings.
   - **Nutmeg and Clove**, sourced from the Spice Islands (modern-day Indonesia), were highly sought after for their exotic aroma and purported ability to ward off illness.

2. **Spices as Status Symbols**
   In medieval Europe, spices were a luxury accessible only to the wealthy. The use of these ingredients in baked goods like gingerbread was a display of affluence and sophistication, as well as a nod to their symbolic significance.

3. **Spices in Religious and Cultural Rituals**

   Many spices were used in religious ceremonies and cultural rituals. For example, cinnamon was burned as incense in temples, and ginger was incorporated into Ayurvedic practices. These traditions imbued spices with an air of sacredness that carried over into their culinary applications.

The Mystical Properties of Gingerbread Spices

Each spice in gingerbread carries its own symbolic and mystical associations, making the blend a powerful alchemical creation.

1. **Ginger: The Fire of Transformation**
   - **Symbolism**: Ginger, with its fiery heat, symbolizes vitality, courage, and transformation. It is associated with the element of fire and is thought to ignite energy and passion.
   - **Mystical Uses**: In folklore, ginger was believed to ward off evil spirits and attract prosperity. It was also used in love spells and rituals to increase confidence and strength.
   - **In Alchemy**: Ginger's warming properties were linked to the process of transformation, making it a key ingredient in alchemical elixirs aimed at purifying the body and soul.

2. **Cinnamon: The Bark of Divine Protection**
   - **Symbolism**: Cinnamon represents protection, spiritual elevation, and abundance. Its sweet, woody scent is associated with the sacred and the eternal.
   - **Mystical Uses**: Often burned as incense, cinnamon was believed to purify spaces, attract wealth, and enhance spiritual connections. It was also used in rituals to promote healing and love.
   - **In Alchemy**: Alchemists valued cinnamon for its association with the sun and its role in balancing the humors, particularly in warming the body during cold winters.

1. **Nutmeg: The Seed of Intuition**
   - **Symbolism**: Nutmeg symbolizes clarity, intuition, and mystery. Its rounded form and complex aroma connect it to the cycles of life and the hidden truths of the universe.
   - **Mystical Uses**: Nutmeg was used in talismans to ward off negative energies and enhance psychic abilities. It was also believed to bring luck and clarity to those who carried or consumed it.
   - **In Alchemy**: Nutmeg's dual nature—both intoxicating and grounding—made it a symbol of balance in alchemical practices, representing the union of opposites.
2. **Clove: The Nail of Strength**
   - **Symbolism**: Clove represents strength, endurance, and purification. Its pungent aroma is associated with resilience and fortitude.
   - **Mystical Uses**: Cloves were burned to repel negativity and protect against illness. They were also used in rituals to enhance clarity and resolve.
   - **In Alchemy**: Clove's sharp, penetrating quality was linked to the process of breaking down impurities, making it a key ingredient in purification rituals.
3. **Black Pepper: The Spark of Potential**
   - **Symbolism**: Black pepper, though less commonly associated with sweetness, symbolizes vitality, protection, and transformation.
   - **Mystical Uses**: In ancient rituals, black pepper was used to banish negativity and awaken latent potential. It was considered a spice of action and manifestation.
   - **In Alchemy**: Black pepper's fiery nature aligned it with the element of fire, representing the spark that initiates change and growth.

The Alchemical Roots of Gingerbread Creation

1. **Baking as Alchemy**
   The process of baking gingerbread parallels the principles of alchemy, where raw ingredients undergo transformation through the application of heat. In alchemy, fire is the agent of change, purifying and transmuting base materials into something refined and elevated.
   - **The Ingredients**: The blend of spices in gingerbread represents the harmonious balance of opposites—sweetness and heat, grounding and elevation.
   - **The Dough**: The malleable dough symbolizes raw potential, waiting to be shaped and perfected.
   - **The Oven**: The oven serves as the alchemical crucible, where transformation occurs and the finished creation emerges.

2. **Symbolism in the Shape of Gingerbread**
   Gingerbread figures and houses, with their intricate designs, reflect the alchemical principle of *Solve et Coagula*—the breaking down of components to reassemble them into a perfected whole. Each shape carries meaning, from the unity of a gingerbread house to the individuality of gingerbread figures.

3. **The Role of Intent**
   In both alchemy and baking, intent plays a crucial role. The act of creating gingerbread is not merely physical but also symbolic, with the baker imbuing their creation with care, creativity, and purpose.

Cultural and Spiritual Significance of Gingerbread Spices

1. **A Symbol of Winter Resilience**
   The warming spices in gingerbread are particularly significant during winter, when cold and darkness dominate. Their fiery

qualities represent the triumph of light and warmth over the chill of the season.

2. **A Connection to the Divine**

   The spices in gingerbread have long been associated with sacred rituals and offerings. Their inclusion in a holiday treat elevates gingerbread from a simple confection to a symbol of spiritual connection and gratitude.

3. **A Bridge Between Cultures**

   The global origins of gingerbread spices reflect the interconnectedness of cultures through trade and tradition. By incorporating these ingredients, gingerbread becomes a culinary testament to the blending of diverse influences and shared human experiences.

The Gingerbread Golem: A Confection of Sweet Power

The Gingerbread Golem, as a figure crafted from these alchemically symbolic spices, carries the combined meanings of its ingredients.

1. **Strength in Sweetness**

   The spices in the Gingerbread Golem imbue it with symbolic strength and resilience, making it a powerful protector of the home and traditions.

2. **A Seasonal Alchemical Creation**

   By blending and baking these spices, the Gingerbread Golem becomes an alchemical symbol of transformation, unity, and the triumph of intention over chaos.

3. **A Modern Mythical Confection**

   The Gingerbread Golem's spicy composition connects it to ancient traditions of protection and purification, while its festive form makes it a playful yet profound addition to holiday lore.

Conclusion: The Spiced Heart of Gingerbread's Mysticism

The spices in gingerbread are more than just flavorings—they are carriers of history, symbolism, and mysticism. Each ingredient contributes to the transformative power of gingerbread, elevating it from a simple treat to a creation rich with meaning.

The Gingerbread Golem, as a sentinel crafted from these potent ingredients, embodies the alchemical roots of gingerbread, standing as a symbol of resilience, warmth, and the enduring power of creation. Through its sweet and spiced essence, the Gingerbread Golem reminds us of the deeper connections that define the holiday season, bridging the physical and the spiritual in a fragrant, flavorful union.

Chapter 14: "The Folklore of Fracture: When Gingerbread Crumbles"

In the delicate world of gingerbread creations, there is a sobering truth: the very fragility that makes them charming also makes them vulnerable. A crumbling gingerbread house is more than a holiday mishap; it is a symbolic reminder of the fragility inherent in both physical and metaphorical constructs. Across folklore, the image of crumbling gingerbread serves as a cautionary tale, warning us about the perils of neglect, overreach, and unseen vulnerability.

The Structural Symbolism of Gingerbread

Gingerbread, celebrated for its warm spices and festive association, holds a paradoxical place in folklore. While it represents community, creativity, and celebration, its fragility is a silent but persistent reminder of impermanence. Historically, cultures have used this dichotomy to illustrate deeper truths:

- **Germanic Folklore**: In the tale of *Hansel and Gretel*, the gingerbread house represents both temptation and peril. The structure, seemingly perfect, is a veneer that masks its fragility. When faced with conflict—whether in the form of hungry children or shifting moral dynamics—it is ultimately destroyed.
- **Slavic Traditions**: Gingerbread is tied to tales of community collapse. In one Russian legend, a village built an elaborate gingerbread city to honor their gods. When they failed to maintain it, the city crumbled, and the gods, angered by their neglect, sent famine. The metaphorical message was clear: ignoring foundational care invites destruction.
- **Nordic Myths**: In certain Scandinavian stories, crumbling gingerbread is an omen. A fractured cookie or cake signifies upcoming hardship or betrayal, often reflecting the importance of vigilance in maintaining family and community bonds.

Metaphor of Fracture: Lessons in Vulnerability

The concept of gingerbread crumbling transcends its culinary roots, becoming a broader metaphor for human fragility. Whether in relationships, organizations, or personal resilience, the image is a stark reminder of the consequences of neglect or imbalance.

1. **Structural Weakness**

   Gingerbread structures are inherently fragile due to their design and materials. The same is true of endeavors built on shaky foundations. This serves as a metaphor for:
   - Poor planning or lack of foresight in personal or professional projects.
   - Relationships that, while sweet, lack the depth or resilience to withstand external pressures.

2. **Neglect and Decay**

   Like a gingerbread house left too long on display, anything left uncared for will eventually crumble. Neglect in maintaining structures—be they physical, emotional, or societal—leads to inevitable decline. The folklore teaches:
   - Proactive care and maintenance are essential for longevity.
   - Even the strongest bonds or achievements can weaken if left unattended.

3. **The Domino Effect**

   When one part of a gingerbread house fails—be it a wall, roof, or foundation—the entire structure is at risk. This is a clear metaphor for how interconnected vulnerabilities can lead to systemic collapse:
   - A single ignored flaw in an organization can unravel its stability.
   - Minor cracks in communication or trust within relationships can cascade into irreparable rifts.

Lessons from Crumbling Gingerbread in Modern Contexts

Modern reinterpretations of this folklore emphasize the importance of mindfulness and resilience:

- **In Leadership**: A leader must identify and address weak points before they become critical failures. The folklore serves as a reminder to build with both strength and flexibility.
- **In Personal Growth**: The metaphor of crumbling gingerbread inspires self-reflection. Identifying one's own "cracks"—whether they be emotional, physical, or spiritual—allows for growth and fortification.
- **In Society**: Social and communal structures, much like gingerbread houses, are held together by mutual care and understanding. When divisions arise, the whole can crumble. This metaphor underlines the need for empathy and collaboration.

Reinforcing Resilience: Learning from Folklore

To counter the vulnerabilities symbolized by a crumbling gingerbread house, we must adopt practices of intentional reinforcement. Lessons from folklore offer guidance:

- **Balance in Design**: Gingerbread, like life, thrives when balance is prioritized. Overloading a house with decorations may lead to collapse, just as taking on too much in life can lead to burnout.
- **Adaptability**: Reinforcing gingerbread structures with additional supports—royal icing or edible dowels—mirrors the human need for adaptability. Flexibility allows us to weather unexpected challenges.
- **Community Effort**: Many traditional gingerbread projects were communal endeavors, reflecting the importance of shared responsibility. Collaboration strengthens both literal and metaphorical structures.

A Warning and a Promise

While the folklore of crumbling gingerbread serves as a warning, it also offers hope. Fragility is not failure; it is a natural state that invites care and consideration. The act of rebuilding—a collapsed wall, a broken bond, or a fragile dream—is as much a part of the human experience as the joy of initial creation.

In embracing the vulnerability of gingerbread, we learn to approach all of life's endeavors with humility, mindfulness, and a touch of sweet determination. A fractured gingerbread house reminds us that strength is not in avoiding collapse, but in our ability to rebuild with even greater care.

Chapter 15: "The Shadow Archetype: Embracing Darkness in Holiday Myths"

Holidays are often viewed as times of joy, celebration, and togetherness. Yet, beneath the surface of festive cheer lies a hidden dimension—one that is darker, more introspective, and deeply symbolic. Applying Jungian philosophy, we uncover the **Shadow Archetype**, a concept that reveals the unacknowledged and repressed aspects of the psyche. When we view the Gingerbread Golem through this lens, it becomes a profound metaphor for the duality of holiday traditions and the need to embrace the darkness that coexists with the light.

The Shadow Archetype: A Jungian Framework

In Carl Jung's psychological theory, the **Shadow** is the part of the unconscious mind that contains the aspects of ourselves we find undesirable, shameful, or difficult to confront. Far from being purely negative, the Shadow is an integral part of the psyche that, when integrated, leads to wholeness. Without it, our view of ourselves—and the world—remains incomplete.

The Gingerbread Golem, with its sweet exterior and ominous undertones, is an ideal embodiment of the Shadow during the holiday season. It represents the tension between external appearances of joy and the internal complexities of human emotion. By examining its shadow side, we can understand the myths that challenge the holiday ideal and allow space for growth, authenticity, and balance.

Gingerbread as Dual Symbolism

Gingerbread, like the holidays themselves, is a paradox. It is warm and comforting, yet it is also fragile and impermanent. The Gingerbread Golem reflects this duality:

1. **The Light Side**

   The Gingerbread Golem, in its wholesome form, symbolizes creativity, nourishment, and celebration. It is a festive creation, tied to community, family, and joy. Yet, this perfection often masks deeper truths.

2. **The Shadow Side**

   The darker aspect of the Gingerbread Golem emerges when it crumbles, decays, or becomes menacing in folklore. In this form, it serves as a warning of excess, impermanence, and the dangers of unchecked indulgence. The shadow of the Golem reminds us that:

   - Excessive sweetness can lead to decay, mirroring the hollowness that sometimes accompanies forced cheer.
   - The constructed perfection of holidays may crumble under the weight of unrealistic expectations.

The Gingerbread Golem as a Mirror of the Human Psyche

Holiday myths involving the Gingerbread Golem often act as mirrors, reflecting the inner struggles we experience during the season. These tales explore themes of repression, fear, and transformation. By applying Jungian principles, we can decode these stories:

1. **The Shadow of Perfection**

   Holidays often come with societal pressure to create a picture-perfect experience. The Gingerbread Golem, with its intricately decorated surface, represents the idealized facade we strive to maintain. Its shadow emerges when the facade begins to crack:
   - Emotional strain and unmet expectations creep in, exposing vulnerabilities.
   - The Golem's shadow warns against losing oneself in external appearances while neglecting internal authenticity.

2. **The Shadow of Excess**

   The Gingerbread Golem's abundance of sweetness can tip into overindulgence, symbolizing the darker side of consumption during the holidays. This shadow highlights:
   - The unsustainable nature of materialism and its impact on emotional well-being.
   - The emptiness that follows when we focus on excess rather than substance.

3. **The Shadow of Repression**

   Holiday traditions often suppress darker emotions, encouraging people to "keep the peace" or "stay cheerful." The Gingerbread Golem's shadow, however, reminds us that:

- Ignoring sadness, frustration, or anxiety doesn't eliminate them; it pushes them into the unconscious, where they grow more powerful.
- Confronting and integrating these feelings leads to deeper understanding and a more balanced experience.

Holiday Myths and the Shadow

Across cultures, holiday myths often feature characters or elements that embody the Shadow Archetype. These figures are not purely antagonistic; they serve as teachers, challengers, and reminders of what lies beneath the surface:

1. **Krampus**
   The dark counterpart to Saint Nicholas, Krampus punishes the naughty, serving as a symbol of discipline and balance. Like the Gingerbread Golem's shadow, Krampus reminds us that holidays are not just about rewards but also about reflection and accountability.

2. **The Yule Cat (Icelandic Myth)**
   This monstrous feline devours those who do not receive new clothes for the holidays. Its shadow symbolism warns against complacency and neglect, urging preparation and effort.

3. **The Gingerbread Golem**
   In its shadow form, the Gingerbread Golem becomes a cautionary figure. Its sweetness turns saccharine, its structure crumbles under pressure, and it reveals the consequences of neglecting emotional or spiritual foundations during the holidays.

Embracing the Shadow: Lessons from the Gingerbread Golem

Jungian philosophy teaches that wholeness is achieved not by avoiding the Shadow, but by integrating it. To embrace the Gingerbread Golem's shadow side is to acknowledge the hidden truths of the holiday season and to grow from them. Here's how:

1. **Confronting Expectations**

   The holidays are rife with unrealistic expectations—of joy, harmony, and perfection. The Gingerbread Golem's shadow encourages us to:
   - Recognize that imperfection is natural and human.
   - Let go of the need for everything to go "just right" and find beauty in authenticity.

2. **Acknowledging Emotions**

   The season often demands a forced happiness that denies the complexity of human emotion. The Golem's shadow reminds us to:
   - Create space for grief, frustration, or loneliness alongside celebration.
   - See these feelings not as weaknesses but as part of a full emotional spectrum.

3. **Balancing Light and Dark**

   Integrating the Shadow means finding balance. Just as the Golem represents both creativity and decay, we can embrace both joy and solemnity, light and dark. This balance creates a more meaningful and grounded experience.

Reclaiming the Shadow in Holiday Traditions

Incorporating the lessons of the Shadow Archetype into holiday rituals can lead to a richer, more fulfilling celebration. Ideas for embracing the Gingerbread Golem's shadow include:

- **Creative Destruction**
  Build a gingerbread structure with the intent of breaking it down at the end of the season. Use the act of destruction as a symbolic release of the year's burdens or failures, allowing space for renewal.
- **Reflection Rituals**
  Include moments of quiet introspection in your holiday routine. Journaling or meditation can help explore the emotions and challenges that arise during the season.
- **Symbolic Offerings**
  Craft or bake something imperfect on purpose as an offering to the shadow side of the holidays. This act acknowledges the beauty in flaws and the necessity of imperfection.

Conclusion: The Sweetness of Shadows

The Gingerbread Golem, when viewed through the lens of the Shadow Archetype, becomes more than a festive creation; it is a profound reminder of our dual nature. By embracing its shadow, we learn to see the holidays—and ourselves—with greater depth and authenticity. The darkness within the season does not diminish its light; instead, it enhances it, allowing us to experience the full spectrum of what it means to celebrate, reflect, and grow.

Chapter 16: "Cultural Reflections: Global Holiday Guardians and Terrors"

The holidays are a time of joy, community, and storytelling, but woven into festive traditions around the world are figures that serve as both protectors and harbingers of fear. These beings reflect the complexities of human nature, embodying not only light and celebration but also shadows and cautionary lessons. The Gingerbread Golem, with its dual nature of sweetness and menace, finds its place among a diverse pantheon of **holiday guardians and terrors** from cultures across the globe. By comparing the Golem to these figures, we can understand the universal need for archetypes that inspire both reverence and reflection.

The Role of Holiday Archetypes

Holiday figures serve several functions in cultural storytelling:

1. **Guardians**: Protectors of traditions, moral values, and communal harmony.
2. **Terrors**: Cautionary figures that enforce discipline, warn against excess, or challenge societal norms.
3. **Dual Archetypes**: Beings who embody both light and dark, illustrating the balance necessary for growth and survival.

The Gingerbread Golem, with its potential to crumble or become menacing, aligns with this third archetype. It reminds us that even in celebration, there is a need for vigilance and introspection.

Comparative Analysis: Global Holiday Guardians and Terrors
1. Krampus (Central Europe)

- **Description**: A goat-like figure with horns, Krampus is the shadow counterpart to Saint Nicholas. While Nicholas rewards good behavior, Krampus punishes the naughty by whipping them or taking them away in his sack.
- **Cultural Role**: Krampus is a terrifying reminder that rewards are balanced by consequences. His presence during holiday parades ensures that morality and discipline are not forgotten in the festivities.
- **Comparison to the Gingerbread Golem**: Like Krampus, the Gingerbread Golem serves as a cautionary figure, warning against neglect or indulgence. Both embody the consequences of ignoring underlying issues—whether moral or structural.

2. The Yule Lads (Iceland)

- **Description**: Thirteen mischievous trolls who visit children in the days leading up to Christmas. Each has a unique name and behavior, such as "Spoon-Licker" or "Window-Peeper." They leave gifts for well-behaved children and rotting potatoes for the disobedient.
- **Cultural Role**: The Yule Lads bring a playful but unsettling energy to the season, blurring the line between guardian and terror. Their antics serve as both entertainment and a reminder to behave.
- **Comparison to the Gingerbread Golem**: The Golem, like the Yule Lads, occupies a liminal space between humor and fear. Its crumbling form or potential menace reflects the unpredictability and fragility of holiday traditions.

3. The Yule Cat (Iceland)

- **Description**: A monstrous feline that devours those who fail to receive new clothes before Christmas.
- **Cultural Role**: The Yule Cat enforces a sense of preparedness and industriousness. It is a stark reminder that the holidays are not only about indulgence but also about readiness and effort.
- **Comparison to the Gingerbread Golem**: The Yule Cat's looming threat mirrors the Gingerbread Golem's shadow side. Both figures highlight the dangers of complacency and the need to uphold holiday rituals with care and intention.

4. Père Fouettard (France)

- **Description**: "Father Whipper," a sinister companion of Saint Nicholas, is tasked with punishing misbehaving children. Often depicted as a bearded man in dark robes, Père Fouettard symbolizes retribution and accountability.
- **Cultural Role**: Père Fouettard ensures that the moral lessons of the holiday season are upheld. His presence emphasizes the duality of reward and punishment.
- **Comparison to the Gingerbread Golem**: While Père Fouettard enforces moral discipline, the Gingerbread Golem enforces structural and emotional discipline. Both remind us that neglect—whether of behavior or of deeper vulnerabilities—leads to consequences.

5. Mari Lwyd (Wales)

- **Description**: A skeletal horse figure draped in a white sheet, Mari Lwyd is part of a wassailing tradition. Groups carrying Mari Lwyd go door-to-door singing and challenging homeowners to verbal battles.
- **Cultural Role**: Mari Lwyd represents both a challenge and a blessing. Its eerie appearance contrasts with the joy of song and community, creating a balance between the unsettling and the celebratory.
- **Comparison to the Gingerbread Golem**: Mari Lwyd and the Gingerbread Golem both juxtapose light and dark. The Golem's sweet exterior and potential menace parallel Mari Lwyd's combination of haunting imagery and communal bonding.

6. La Befana (Italy)

- **Description**: An old witch who delivers gifts to children on Epiphany Eve. La Befana is kind but stern, rewarding good behavior with gifts and bad behavior with coal or ashes.
- **Cultural Role**: La Befana embodies wisdom and justice. She bridges the light and dark aspects of the holiday season, showing that kindness is paired with accountability.
- **Comparison to the Gingerbread Golem**: Like La Befana, the Gingerbread Golem is a figure of balance. Its structural fragility and potential danger serve as reminders that joy must be rooted in responsibility.

7. The Nisse (Scandinavia)

- **Description**: Small, gnome-like beings who protect farms and homes during the winter. However, if disrespected or neglected, they can turn mischievous or even vengeful.
- **Cultural Role**: Nisse represent the importance of gratitude and respect for the unseen forces that sustain us. Their dual nature—protective yet potentially dangerous—reflects the balance of light and dark in holiday traditions.
- **Comparison to the Gingerbread Golem**: The Nisse's reaction to neglect mirrors the Gingerbread Golem's warning against carelessness. Both figures emphasize the need to honor traditions and maintain vigilance.

The Universal Need for Holiday Guardians and Terrors

The existence of figures like the Gingerbread Golem and its counterparts across cultures reveals a shared human instinct to explore the darker side of celebration. These archetypes serve several purposes:

1. **Teaching Morality**: Figures like Krampus and Père Fouettard reinforce the importance of ethical behavior, using fear as a tool for instruction.
2. **Highlighting Vulnerability**: The fragility of gingerbread or the threat of the Yule Cat reminds us that joy is not guaranteed—it must be earned and maintained.
3. **Balancing Extremes**: Holiday guardians and terrors ensure that excess (whether in indulgence, consumption, or complacency) is tempered with reflection and restraint.
4. **Encouraging Community**: Many of these figures, despite their fearsome nature, ultimately bring people together. The verbal battles of Mari Lwyd or the shared traditions of the Nisse foster connection and collective participation.

Modern Relevance: The Shadow in Today's Holidays

The Gingerbread Golem, like its global counterparts, has much to teach us in the modern world. In an era of materialism and curated perfection, these figures challenge us to:

- Reflect on the true meaning of the holidays.
- Acknowledge and embrace imperfections and vulnerabilities.
- Balance celebration with mindfulness, preparation, and gratitude.

Conclusion: A Shared Mythology of Light and Dark

From the crumbling fragility of the Gingerbread Golem to the menacing presence of Krampus, global holiday figures remind us that joy and fear, light and dark, celebration and caution are all part of the human experience. By embracing these dualities, we not only deepen our understanding of the holidays but also enrich our capacity for growth, resilience, and connection. In the Gingerbread Golem's shadow, we find a mirror reflecting our own complexities—and a guide to navigating them with grace.

Chapter 17: "The Golem's Lesson: Morality in Sweet Myths"

Holiday folklore has long been a vehicle for imparting moral lessons, blending whimsy and caution in ways that resonate with audiences of all ages. The Gingerbread Golem, with its contrasting sweetness and menace, exemplifies how stories rooted in festive traditions serve as allegories for ethical behavior, communal harmony, and personal responsibility. This chapter explores the moral dimensions of holiday myths, focusing on the Gingerbread Golem as a symbol of consequences, balance, and growth, while drawing comparisons to similar sweet-themed folklore across cultures.

Morality Through Myth: Why Sweet Myths Matter

Holiday folklore operates on multiple levels. While it entertains, it also functions as a moral compass, using accessible symbols—like gingerbread—to teach complex lessons. Sweet myths, in particular, are effective because they juxtapose delight with danger, making the moral lessons both memorable and impactful.

1. **The Universal Appeal of Sweetness**
   Sweetness represents joy, indulgence, and celebration, making it a powerful metaphor for life's pleasures. By placing moral lessons in the context of sweets, myths connect with people's innate love for the comforting and the familiar.
2. **The Danger of Overindulgence**
   Sweet myths often highlight the perils of excess. Whether it's eating too much candy or neglecting the discipline needed to create balance, these stories warn against letting pleasure overshadow responsibility.
3. **The Fragility of Sweet Creations**
   The ephemeral nature of sweets—like gingerbread—reflects life's impermanence and the need to cherish and protect what we

value. The Gingerbread Golem, as both a creation and a cautionary figure, embodies this fragility.

The Gingerbread Golem as a Moral Teacher

The Gingerbread Golem's dual nature—both delightful and menacing—provides a framework for teaching moral lessons. Its stories address themes of discipline, creativity, and the consequences of neglect.

1. Responsibility and Care

The Gingerbread Golem is often portrayed as a magical being brought to life through human effort, much like traditional golems in Jewish folklore. Its very existence depends on the care and intention of its creator. Neglect or misuse leads to its transformation from a benign guardian into a destructive force.

- **Lesson**: Responsibility is essential in all acts of creation. Whether it's building relationships, crafting art, or nurturing a community, neglect can turn something beautiful into something harmful.

2. Moderation and Balance

Gingerbread, as a holiday treat, symbolizes indulgence. However, the Golem's tales often caution against overindulgence or imbalance. Excessive sweetness, whether in the form of food or behavior, can lead to decay.

- **Lesson**: Balance is key to maintaining harmony in life. Too much of anything—even something good—can lead to negative outcomes.

3. The Consequences of Greed

In many myths, the Gingerbread Golem is tied to stories of greed or exploitation. For example, characters who consume its sugary components without thought for the consequences often face its wrath.

- **Lesson**: Greed and selfishness disrupt the natural order, leading to personal and communal suffering. Sharing and mindfulness create a better outcome for everyone.

4. The Importance of Intention

Like the traditional golem, the Gingerbread Golem acts according to the intentions of its creator. Pure motives lead to positive outcomes, while selfish or careless actions bring chaos.

- **Lesson**: Intention matters as much as action. Approaching any endeavor with care and respect fosters success and avoids unintended consequences.

Moral Lessons in Sweet Myths Across Cultures

The Gingerbread Golem is not the only sweet-themed figure to convey moral lessons. Across cultures, stories involving sugary treats or creations offer rich allegories for human behavior.

1. The Witch's Gingerbread House (*Hansel and Gretel*, Germany)

- **Moral Lesson**: The witch's gingerbread house represents the danger of temptation and the need for vigilance. It also teaches the value of resourcefulness, as Hansel and Gretel outwit the witch.
- **Comparison**: Like the Gingerbread Golem, the witch's house blends sweetness with menace, showing that appearances can be deceiving.

2. Sugar Skulls (Mexico)

- **Cultural Context**: Used during Día de los Muertos, sugar skulls honor the dead while reminding the living of life's transience.
- **Moral Lesson**: Embrace life fully while acknowledging its impermanence. Respect for tradition and loved ones creates a meaningful existence.
- **Comparison**: The fragility of sugar skulls mirrors the ephemeral nature of the Gingerbread Golem, both teaching the importance of cherishing what we have.

3. Candy Canes (Christian Symbolism)

- **Cultural Context**: Candy canes are often interpreted as symbols of purity (white) and sacrifice (red stripes).
- **Moral Lesson**: Acts of kindness and sacrifice bring joy to others, reflecting the spirit of the holiday season.

- **Comparison**: While the Gingerbread Golem is less overtly benevolent, it also reflects the idea that creation and intention have moral weight.

Holiday Morality: Lessons for Modern Times

The moral teachings embedded in holiday folklore remain deeply relevant. In the case of the Gingerbread Golem, its stories reflect universal truths about human nature and societal dynamics.

1. Ethical Consumption

In an age of materialism, the Gingerbread Golem's lessons about moderation and responsibility are particularly poignant. Overindulgence—whether in food, gifts, or resources—leads to imbalance and eventual decline.

2. Creativity and Accountability

The act of creating something, whether it's a gingerbread house or a community project, comes with responsibility. The Golem's transformation into a destructive force warns against neglecting this responsibility.

3. Embracing Duality

The Gingerbread Golem's dual nature teaches that joy and caution, light and dark, must coexist. By acknowledging both sides of the holiday experience, we can create celebrations that are both meaningful and sustainable.

Practical Applications: Teaching the Golem's Lessons

The Gingerbread Golem's moral teachings can be integrated into modern holiday traditions in ways that are both fun and educational:

1. **Storytelling**

   Share tales of the Gingerbread Golem with children, highlighting its lessons about responsibility, balance, and intention. Adapt the stories to reflect current values and challenges.

2. **Interactive Lessons**

   Create a gingerbread house with a focus on structural integrity and care. Use the process to discuss the importance of attention to detail, teamwork, and patience.

3. **Reflection Rituals**

Incorporate moments of introspection into holiday celebrations. Reflect on the year's actions and intentions, using the Golem's lessons as a framework for personal growth.

Conclusion: Sweet Myths as Guides to a Better World

The Gingerbread Golem, like other sweet-themed holiday figures, serves as a reminder that joy and morality are intertwined. Its stories encourage us to savor life's sweetness without losing sight of our responsibilities and values. By embracing the lessons of the Golem and similar myths, we can create celebrations—and lives—that are both fulfilling and meaningful.

Chapter 18: "The Sweet and the Sinister: Balancing Opposites"

Human traditions are steeped in duality, reflecting an inherent drive to reconcile the opposing forces of light and dark, joy and fear, creation and destruction. This interplay between opposites is not merely an artistic or cultural phenomenon—it is a profound philosophical and psychological truth about the human experience. Holiday myths, such as the Gingerbread Golem, serve as microcosms of this balance, offering insight into why humanity perpetually seeks equilibrium between the sweet and the sinister.

The Philosophical Foundations of Duality

Throughout history, philosophers, theologians, and thinkers have grappled with the concept of duality, recognizing it as a fundamental structure of existence. The Gingerbread Golem, with its sugary charm and potential menace, exemplifies this philosophical framework, echoing ancient wisdom about balance and the necessity of opposites.

1. Duality in Ancient Philosophy

- **Yin and Yang (Taoism)**: In Taoist philosophy, the universe is governed by two complementary forces—Yin (dark, passive, feminine) and Yang (light, active, masculine). Harmony arises from their balance, not the dominance of one over the other. The Gingerbread Golem mirrors this interplay: its sweetness (Yang) is incomplete without the lurking shadow of its fragility or potential menace (Yin).

- **Heraclitus (Greek Philosophy)**: Heraclitus emphasized that conflict and contrast drive the world's order. "Strife is justice," he argued, suggesting that opposites define and sustain each other. The sweet and sinister aspects of holiday myths follow this logic, as joy is heightened by an awareness of its fragility.

2. Psychological Perspectives on Opposites

- **Carl Jung's Shadow Archetype**: Jung's concept of the Shadow explains the human need to confront and integrate the darker aspects of the psyche. Holiday myths, like the Gingerbread Golem, externalize this tension, allowing people to explore the darker side of themselves in a safe, symbolic context.
- **Sigmund Freud's Pleasure Principle vs. Reality Principle**: Freud argued that human behavior is shaped by the tension between seeking pleasure and acknowledging reality. Holiday traditions—sweet and sinister—reflect this dichotomy, providing both indulgence and caution.

Holiday Traditions as Reflections of Duality

Holiday myths from around the world reveal a shared cultural effort to balance opposites. These traditions do not shy away from darkness; instead, they weave it into celebrations, ensuring that joy is grounded in meaning.

1. Sweetness as a Celebration of Life

- Festive treats like gingerbread are symbolic of life's pleasures. Their sweetness represents abundance, connection, and the warmth of communal bonds.
- The ephemeral nature of sweets reminds us to savor the present moment, as joy, like a delicate gingerbread creation, is fleeting.

2. The Sinister as a Warning

- Darkness in holiday myths serves to temper indulgence. Figures like the Gingerbread Golem, Krampus, or the Yule Cat act as moral correctives, ensuring that celebration does not tip into excess or carelessness.
- The sinister elements underscore vulnerability—whether to external threats, internal flaws, or the inevitable passage of time.

3. Balancing Sweet and Sinister

- By juxtaposing sweetness with menace, traditions create a holistic experience. The joy of a well-built gingerbread house is heightened by the knowledge that it could crumble, just as the presence of Krampus makes Saint Nicholas's kindness more profound.
- This balance reflects a universal truth: light shines brightest against darkness.

Why Humanity Seeks Balance

Humanity's desire to balance opposites is rooted in both practical and existential needs. The integration of light and dark in traditions serves several purposes:

1. Psychological Integration

- Confronting darkness in a controlled, symbolic way—through myths, rituals, or storytelling—allows individuals and societies to process fear, loss, and uncertainty.
- The Gingerbread Golem's dual nature invites introspection, helping us reconcile the sweetness we seek with the fragility and responsibility inherent in life.

2. Ethical and Moral Lessons

- Holiday myths use the interplay of opposites to teach moral lessons. The Gingerbread Golem, for example, cautions against neglect, overindulgence, and superficiality, encouraging balance in both action and intention.
- These stories remind us that life is not simply about pursuing pleasure but also about acknowledging and addressing its consequences.

3. Community Cohesion

- The shared experience of balancing sweet and sinister elements in traditions fosters a sense of collective identity. Celebrating together—whether by building a gingerbread house or recounting its potential collapse—reinforces communal bonds.

4. Existential Reassurance

- Duality in myths mirrors the duality of life itself: creation and destruction, growth and decay, life and death. By embracing this duality, humanity finds comfort in the cyclical nature of existence.

Case Study: The Gingerbread Golem as a Symbol of Balance
The Gingerbread Golem exemplifies humanity's quest for balance through its dual symbolism:

- **Sweetness**: The Golem begins as a delightful creation, embodying joy, creativity, and the warmth of holiday traditions.
- **Sinister Potential**: As its stories unfold, the Golem reveals a darker side, symbolizing fragility, consequences, and the dangers of neglect or hubris.

The tension between these aspects reflects broader human truths:

- The sweetness of life is fleeting and must be cherished.
- Darkness is not to be feared but understood, as it provides depth and perspective.

Balancing Opposites in Modern Traditions

In contemporary celebrations, the sweet and the sinister continue to coexist, offering opportunities to reflect on duality:

1. Halloween and Christmas Crossover

- Modern culture increasingly blends the macabre with the festive, as seen in films like *The Nightmare Before Christmas*. This fusion reflects an acknowledgment that joy and fear are intertwined.

2. Sweet Treats with Symbolic Depth

- Treats like gingerbread houses or sugar cookies carry deeper meanings when paired with cautionary tales. The act of creating these delicacies becomes a ritual of balance, blending indulgence with mindfulness.

3. Reflection and Renewal

- Traditions like New Year's resolutions mirror the balance of opposites: the joy of celebration is paired with a sober commitment to improvement.

Practical Applications: Living the Lesson of Balance

The philosophical insights of the Gingerbread Golem and similar myths can inform daily life:

1. **Embrace Duality**: Recognize that light and dark, joy and sorrow, coexist. Accepting both leads to a fuller, richer experience.
2. **Practice Moderation**: Whether in holiday celebrations or daily routines, strive for balance. Indulge, but not to excess; celebrate, but with mindfulness.
3. **Create with Care**: Like building a gingerbread house, approach all endeavors with intention and respect for their fragility.

Conclusion: The Beauty of Balance

The sweet and the sinister are not adversaries but partners in a dance that defines human existence. Holiday traditions, like the story of the Gingerbread Golem, remind us that balance is not a fixed state but an ongoing process. By acknowledging and integrating opposites, we create a life—and a world—that is both meaningful and whole. Through the lens of sweetness and menace, light and dark, we come to understand not just the holidays, but ourselves.

Chapter 19: "The Gingerbread Golem in Modern Media"

The Gingerbread Golem, a symbol of sweetness intertwined with menace, offers a fascinating archetype for adaptation in modern media. Its dual nature—both delightful and foreboding—presents an opportunity to explore themes of creation, vulnerability, and morality in compelling ways. While this figure is rooted in folklore, its potential for storytelling across genres like film, television, literature, and gaming is vast. This chapter examines how the Gingerbread Golem has appeared in pop culture and proposes new ways it could be adapted to resonate with contemporary audiences.

Existing Representations in Pop Culture

Although the Gingerbread Golem is not as well-known as other folkloric figures, its concept has inspired several interpretations in modern media. These examples showcase its versatility and the wide range of themes it can embody.

1. The Gingerbread Man in Horror

- **Example**: *The Gingerdead Man* (2005)
  This low-budget horror film turns the Gingerbread Man into a malevolent force, combining campy humor with slasher tropes. While the film lacks the depth of folklore, it demonstrates the potential for the Gingerbread Golem to inhabit the horror genre, leveraging its uncanny contrast between sweetness and menace.

2. The Gingerbread Man in Animation

- **Example**: *Shrek* series
  The character Gingy offers a comedic take on the gingerbread archetype, blending innocence with moments of unexpected boldness. While not a Golem per se, Gingy hints at the latent potential for gingerbread figures to express deeper themes, such as resilience and defiance.

3. Gingerbread in Holiday Narratives

- **Example**: *The Nutcracker and the Four Realms* (2018)
  While not explicitly about a Gingerbread Golem, this film incorporates gingerbread soldiers and holiday magic. These elements suggest how gingerbread creations can play a role in fantastical worlds, offering whimsy alongside conflict.

Potential Adaptations: Exploring the Golem's Narrative Depth

The Gingerbread Golem's rich symbolism makes it an ideal candidate for reinterpretation in a variety of genres. Below are detailed concepts for how this archetype could be adapted into modern media.

1. Fantasy: The Protector Turned Monster

- **Plot**: In a magical kingdom, bakers create a Gingerbread Golem to defend their village from marauding invaders. Initially a loyal protector, the Golem begins to crumble due to neglect and eventually becomes a threat, forcing the villagers to confront their own failings.
- **Themes**: Responsibility, the fragility of creation, and the consequences of neglect.
- **Medium**: A novel series or animated film targeting a young adult audience.

2. Horror: The Sweetness of Terror

- **Plot**: A family tradition of baking gingerbread houses takes a dark turn when a vengeful spirit inhabits the dough. The Gingerbread Golem rises, enacting poetic justice against those who exploit holiday cheer for selfish gain.
- **Themes**: Greed, familial tension, and the haunting of holiday excess.
- **Medium**: A feature-length horror movie or a Netflix holiday special with a sinister twist.

3. Comedy: The Accidental Golem

- **Plot**: A hapless baker accidentally brings a Gingerbread Golem to life using a magical recipe. The Golem, sweet but mischievous, wreaks havoc in the town, forcing the baker to team up with unlikely allies to contain its chaos.
- **Themes**: The humor of unintended consequences and the importance of community.
- **Medium**: An animated family film in the vein of *Hotel Transylvania*.

4. Science Fiction: A Post-Apocalyptic Golem

- **Plot**: In a dystopian future where food scarcity reigns, scientists develop edible sentinels to protect their resources. A Gingerbread Golem, created as a test subject, gains sentience and questions its purpose, oscillating between defending humanity and seeking freedom.
- **Themes**: The ethics of creation, artificial intelligence, and survival.
- **Medium**: A graphic novel or sci-fi streaming series.

5. Gaming: A Playable Holiday Monster

- **Concept**: The Gingerbread Golem is introduced as a playable character or antagonist in a holiday-themed expansion of a popular game. Players must craft, battle, or ally with the Golem, depending on its alignment.
- **Themes**: Strategy, teamwork, and the balance between creation and destruction.
- **Medium**: Video games like *Fortnite*, *World of Warcraft*, or *Genshin Impact*.

Core Themes for Adaptation

To successfully adapt the Gingerbread Golem, storytellers must emphasize the universal themes that make it compelling:

1. Fragility and Strength

- The Golem's vulnerability—both physical (it crumbles) and emotional (it responds to neglect)—offers a poignant metaphor for human frailty and resilience.
- This theme resonates in narratives about personal growth, societal responsibility, and the cost of hubris.

2. The Duality of Sweetness and Menace

- The Gingerbread Golem's sugary exterior contrasts with its potential for danger, reflecting humanity's capacity for both kindness and cruelty.
- This duality lends itself to stories that explore ethical dilemmas, such as the consequences of exploiting or overindulging in life's pleasures.

3. Creation and Responsibility

- As a crafted being, the Golem represents the responsibility that comes with creation—be it art, technology, or relationships.
- This theme is particularly relevant in modern discussions about artificial intelligence, environmental sustainability, and parenting.

4. Seasonal Morality Tales

- Holiday traditions often blend joy with cautionary lessons, making the Gingerbread Golem a perfect vehicle for exploring themes of moderation, gratitude, and community.

The Gingerbread Golem's Role in Cultural Commentary

Modern media adaptations of the Gingerbread Golem could serve as allegories for contemporary issues:

1. Consumerism and Materialism

- A story about the Golem could critique holiday overindulgence, exploring how the pursuit of perfection (in decorations, gifts, or experiences) leads to unintended consequences.

2. Climate Change and Sustainability

- The fragility of the Gingerbread Golem could symbolize the precariousness of the planet, emphasizing the importance of care and responsibility in preserving what we create.

3. AI and Ethical Creation

- In a sci-fi context, the Golem could parallel debates about the ethics of artificial intelligence, exploring what happens when a creation exceeds its intended purpose.

Future Potential: Expanding the Golem's Mythos

To ensure the Gingerbread Golem's continued relevance, creators could expand its mythology:

1. **Origin Stories**: Explore the ritual or magic behind its creation, grounding the Golem in a rich cultural or historical context.
2. **Crossover Narratives**: Pair the Golem with other holiday figures (e.g., Krampus, Santa Claus) to create shared universes of holiday lore.
3. **Merchandising and Spin-Offs**: Develop toys, games, and collectibles that bring the Golem into mainstream pop culture, ensuring its place alongside iconic holiday figures.

Conclusion: A Sweet Future for a Sinister Myth

The Gingerbread Golem's unique blend of sweetness and menace makes it a versatile and enduring archetype for modern media. Whether as a protector, a monster, or a philosophical symbol, it reflects humanity's eternal quest to balance light and dark. By embracing the Golem's potential, creators can craft stories that are both entertaining and thought-provoking, ensuring its place in the ever-evolving landscape of pop culture.

Chapter 20: "A Sweet Legacy: The Enduring Symbol of Gingerbread in Folklore"

Gingerbread, a holiday staple with a history as rich as its flavor, has transcended its culinary roots to become a powerful cultural and mythological symbol. Its delicate balance of sweetness and spice mirrors the complexity of the human experience, while its associations with craftsmanship and creativity evoke timeless themes of tradition, community, and morality. The Gingerbread Golem, as an archetype, epitomizes these qualities, weaving together light and dark, joy and caution, to reveal deeper truths about the holidays and humanity itself.

This chapter explores the enduring appeal of gingerbread in folklore and its darker mythological counterparts, examining why this sweet yet fragile medium continues to captivate the imagination.

The Historical Significance of Gingerbread
1. A Culinary Tradition with Deep Roots

- **Origins**: Gingerbread dates back to ancient times, with early versions made from honey and spices. By the Middle Ages, gingerbread had become associated with celebrations and festive occasions in Europe, particularly during the Christmas season.
- **Symbolism**: The spices in gingerbread—particularly ginger, cinnamon, and nutmeg—were once rare and precious, symbolizing wealth and abundance. Its sweetness offered a literal and metaphorical taste of joy, while its intricate decorations reflected artistry and devotion.

2. A Medium for Storytelling

- **Early Forms**: Gingerbread figures and houses were crafted not just as treats but as narrative devices, depicting saints, folklore characters, or biblical scenes.
- **Evolving Myths**: Over time, gingerbread evolved into a storytelling medium in its own right, inspiring tales like *Hansel and*

Gretel, where the enchanted gingerbread house serves as both a lure and a warning.

3. A Global Presence

- Gingerbread traditions are found worldwide, from the intricately designed *lebkuchen* of Germany to the spicy *gingerbread men* popularized in England. Across cultures, it symbolizes warmth, festivity, and a connection to the past.

The Dual Nature of Gingerbread in Folklore

The sweetness of gingerbread is often contrasted with darker undertones in myths and stories. This duality is key to its enduring power as a symbol.

1. Sweetness: Joy and Celebration

- **Communal Bonding**: The act of baking and sharing gingerbread fosters a sense of togetherness, making it a symbol of community and goodwill.
- **Creativity and Craftsmanship**: Gingerbread houses, with their intricate designs, celebrate human ingenuity and the joy of creation.
- **Nostalgia and Comfort**: For many, gingerbread evokes childhood memories of holidays past, connecting the present to a cherished personal and cultural history.

2. Darkness: Fragility and Caution

- **Impermanence**: The delicate, crumbly nature of gingerbread serves as a reminder of life's transience and the need to cherish the moment.
- **Moral Lessons**: Myths involving gingerbread often carry cautionary messages, such as the dangers of overindulgence, greed, or neglect.
- **Mystery and Menace**: Figures like the Gingerbread Golem embody the potential for sweetness to turn sinister, reflecting the shadows that lurk beneath the surface of even the brightest celebrations.

The Gingerbread Golem as a Symbol of Balance

The Gingerbread Golem encapsulates the duality of gingerbread in folklore, embodying both its light and dark aspects. It serves as a microcosm of humanity's struggle to balance joy with responsibility, indulgence with restraint, and creation with destruction.

1. A Reflection of Human Nature

- The Golem's duality mirrors the complexities of human behavior. Its sweetness represents creativity, community, and generosity, while its potential menace warns of the consequences of neglect or excess.

2. A Moral Compass

- Like other mythological figures, the Gingerbread Golem teaches lessons about ethical behavior, emphasizing the importance of care, intention, and mindfulness in all acts of creation.

3. A Reminder of Fragility

- The Golem's vulnerability to crumbling underscores the impermanence of material creations and the need to value what truly matters—relationships, traditions, and shared experiences.

Why Gingerbread Endures as a Holiday Symbol

Gingerbread's enduring appeal lies in its ability to adapt to changing times while retaining its core symbolism. Whether in the form of festive treats, artistic creations, or cautionary tales, gingerbread continues to resonate because it speaks to universal human experiences.

1. Timeless Themes

- Gingerbread represents balance, community, and creativity—values that remain relevant across generations and cultures.
- Its dual nature allows it to address both the joy and challenges of life, making it a meaningful symbol for the holiday season.

2. A Medium for Connection

- The act of baking and decorating gingerbread fosters connection, whether among family members, friends, or entire communities. It is a tradition that bridges the gap between past and present, linking individuals to their cultural and personal histories.

3. Adaptability

- Gingerbread's versatility has allowed it to thrive in diverse forms, from humble cookies to elaborate houses, from festive treats to characters in folklore and media. Its adaptability ensures its continued relevance in a rapidly changing world.

The Legacy of Gingerbread in Modern Culture

In today's world, gingerbread remains a beloved holiday icon, inspiring new traditions, stories, and artistic expressions. Its symbolism continues to evolve, finding new ways to reflect the complexities of the human experience.

1. Gingerbread as an Art Form

- Competitive gingerbread house-making has become a global phenomenon, showcasing the medium's potential for innovation and creativity.
- Gingerbread sculptures and installations push the boundaries of what this humble medium can achieve, blending artistry with tradition.

2. Gingerbread in Storytelling

- Modern adaptations of gingerbread myths, like the Gingerbread Golem, offer fresh perspectives on old themes, addressing contemporary concerns such as sustainability, ethics, and the balance between consumption and conservation.

3. Gingerbread as a Metaphor

- Beyond its physical form, gingerbread serves as a metaphor for the fragility and sweetness of life, reminding us to approach the world with care, gratitude, and imagination.

Conclusion: A Sweet Legacy

The enduring symbol of gingerbread in folklore and culture lies in its ability to balance opposites: the sweet and the sinister, joy and caution, creation and decay. The Gingerbread Golem, as a modern mythological figure, encapsulates this legacy, offering lessons about responsibility, balance, and the fragility of life.

As we continue to celebrate the holidays, gingerbread serves as a reminder of the deeper truths that underpin our traditions. Its sweetness brings joy, its fragility inspires care, and its mythology invites us to reflect on the light and dark within ourselves and our world. In the Gingerbread Golem and its many counterparts, we find a symbol that is both timeless and profoundly human—a legacy as enduring as the stories we tell and the traditions we cherish.

Appendices

Appendix A: Recipes and Rituals

Traditional Gingerbread Recipes and Symbolic Rituals for Crafting Your Own "Golem"

The act of crafting gingerbread—whether as a simple cookie or a complex house—has long been a cherished tradition. It is not merely a culinary endeavor but a symbolic one, blending creativity, intention, and shared experience. This appendix provides time-honored gingerbread recipes and rituals to imbue your creations with deeper meaning. By following these steps, you can create your own "Golem" to honor the balance between light and dark, sweet and sinister, that gingerbread represents.

Traditional Gingerbread Recipes

1. Classic Spiced Gingerbread Dough

This versatile recipe can be used for cookies, houses, or your own Gingerbread Golem. The spices are key to invoking warmth and festive cheer.

Ingredients:

- 3 1/4 cups (425g) all-purpose flour
- 3/4 teaspoon baking soda
- 1 tablespoon ground ginger
- 1 tablespoon ground cinnamon
- 1/2 teaspoon ground cloves
- 1/4 teaspoon ground nutmeg
- 1/2 teaspoon salt
- 1/2 cup (115g) unsalted butter, softened
- 1/2 cup (100g) brown sugar, packed
- 2/3 cup (160ml) molasses
- 1 large egg
- 1 teaspoon vanilla extract

Instructions:

1. Prepare Dry Ingredients: In a large bowl, whisk together flour, baking soda, spices, and salt. Set aside.
2. Cream Butter and Sugar: In a separate bowl, cream the softened butter and brown sugar until light and fluffy.
3. Add Wet Ingredients: Mix in the molasses, egg, and vanilla until fully incorporated.
4. Combine: Gradually add the dry ingredients to the wet mixture, mixing until a smooth dough forms.
5. Chill: Divide the dough into two portions, flatten into disks, wrap in plastic, and refrigerate for at least 2 hours (or overnight).
6. Roll and Shape: Roll out the dough on a floured surface to your desired thickness (1/4 inch for cookies or 1/8 inch for houses). Use cookie cutters or a template for your Golem.
7. Bake: Preheat oven to 350°F (175°C). Place shapes on a parchment-lined baking sheet and bake for 8-12 minutes, depending on size. Let cool completely before decorating.

2. Royal Icing for Decoration and Structure

Royal icing acts as both decoration and "mortar" for constructing gingerbread houses or Golems.

Ingredients:

- 3 cups (375g) powdered sugar, sifted
- 2 large egg whites or 4 tablespoons meringue powder mixed with 6 tablespoons water
- 1/2 teaspoon cream of tartar (optional)
- Food coloring (optional)

Instructions:

1. Whisk: In a clean, grease-free bowl, whisk the egg whites (or meringue powder mixture) until frothy.
2. Mix: Gradually add powdered sugar and cream of tartar, beating until stiff peaks form.
3. Adjust: For piping, use thicker icing; for flooding or smoother finishes, add a few drops of water to thin.
4. Color: Divide and tint with food coloring as desired.

3. Spiced Gingerbread Glaze

A glossy glaze can enhance the appearance and flavor of your Gingerbread Golem.

Ingredients:

- 1 cup (125g) powdered sugar
- 2-3 tablespoons milk or water
- 1/2 teaspoon vanilla or almond extract
- Optional: 1/4 teaspoon ground cinnamon or nutmeg for extra flavor

Instructions:

1. Mix all ingredients until smooth and glossy.
2. Brush or drizzle over baked gingerbread for a shiny finish.

Rituals for Crafting Your Own Gingerbread Golem

The process of creating a Gingerbread Golem can be more than a fun activity—it can become a meaningful ritual that connects you to deeper intentions and holiday traditions.

1. The Ritual of Creation

This ritual focuses on intention-setting and mindfulness during the crafting process.

Purpose: To imbue your Gingerbread Golem with symbolic meaning, reflecting your wishes for the holiday season.

Steps:

1. Gather Supplies: Prepare your gingerbread dough, cutters, decorations, and a quiet space.
2. Set Your Intention: Before rolling out the dough, take a moment to reflect on what you want your Golem to represent (e.g., protection, balance, creativity).
3. Shape Your Golem: As you cut out the shape, visualize the qualities you want to instill in your creation.
4. Bake with Care: Treat the baking process as a metaphor for nurturing your intentions, ensuring the Golem emerges whole and unbroken.
5. Decorate Mindfully: Each decoration can symbolize an attribute (e.g., red for courage, green for growth, gold for prosperity).

2. The Ritual of Protection

Invoke the Gingerbread Golem as a guardian for your home or family.

Purpose: To create a symbolic protector during the holiday season.
Steps:

1. Preparation: Before assembling your Golem, gather additional symbolic items (e.g., cloves for protection, cinnamon sticks for warmth).
2. Incantation: As you assemble your Golem, recite a protective phrase such as:

"From flour and spice, this guardian I make,
To ward off harm and goodwill awake.
With sweetness and strength, it stands by my side,
A beacon of light where shadows reside."

1. Placement: Place your Golem in a central or symbolic location in your home, such as the dining table or mantle.
2. Honor the Golem: Light a candle nearby or share its story with family members to reinforce its presence.

3. The Ritual of Release

At the end of the season, symbolically "release" your Golem to mark a transition.

Purpose: To let go of the year's challenges and prepare for renewal.

Steps:

1. Reflection: Before breaking or dismantling the Golem, reflect on the year's successes and struggles.
2. Symbolic Destruction: Break the Golem gently, symbolizing the release of burdens or old patterns.
3. Share or Compost: Share pieces of the Golem with loved ones (if edible) or compost it as an offering to the earth, closing the cycle of creation and destruction.

Gingerbread as a Symbolic Act

Crafting gingerbread is an act of creativity, care, and connection. Whether you approach it as a casual activity or a profound ritual, the process invites mindfulness and celebration. By integrating traditional recipes with symbolic rituals, you can elevate your holiday traditions, honoring the sweet and sinister legacy of gingerbread in folklore.

Appendix B: The Golem in Comparative Mythology
An Academic Overview of the Golem Archetype Across Cultures

The **golem archetype**—a figure brought to life from inanimate matter—appears across diverse cultural mythologies, reflecting humanity's fascination with creation, power, and responsibility. Though the term "golem" originates in Jewish mysticism, the broader concept of animating lifeless objects is a recurring theme in myths, folklore, and literature worldwide. This appendix examines the golem archetype's evolution, its variations in different cultures, and the universal themes it represents.

1. The Jewish Golem: A Protector and a Warning
Origins and Context:

- The term "golem" derives from the Hebrew word *gelem*, meaning "unformed substance" or "shapeless mass."
- In Jewish mysticism, particularly in the Kabbalistic tradition, the golem is a figure crafted from clay or mud and animated through divine words or sacred rituals.

The Most Famous Golem Story:

- **The Golem of Prague**:
  In this 16th-century legend, Rabbi Judah Loew ben Bezalel created a golem to protect the Jewish community from persecution. The golem, brought to life with the sacred word *emet* ("truth") inscribed on its forehead, became a powerful guardian. However,

when neglected or misused, it grew uncontrollable. Removing the first letter of *emet* to form *met* ("death") deactivated the golem.

Themes:

- **Protection**: The golem was created to defend vulnerable communities, symbolizing the human desire for safety.
- **Hubris and Responsibility**: The golem's destructive potential underscores the dangers of wielding power without accountability.
- **Sacred Knowledge**: The creation of a golem requires divine wisdom, highlighting the delicate balance between human ingenuity and spiritual boundaries.

2. The Homunculus: European Alchemical Tradition
Definition and Context:

- The homunculus is a small, human-like being created artificially, often associated with European alchemy and Renaissance science. It appears in texts such as Paracelsus's writings and Mary Shelley's *Frankenstein*.

Mythological Role:

- **Alchemical Experimentation**: Alchemists sought to mimic divine creation, using mystical and chemical processes to "birth" a homunculus.
- **Moral Questions**: The creation of a homunculus often posed ethical dilemmas about humanity's attempt to play god.

Themes:

- **Creation and Control**: Like the golem, the homunculus represents humanity's yearning to create but also warns of unintended consequences.
- **Knowledge and Hubris**: The homunculus reflects both the potential and peril of human intellect.

3. The Talos of Crete: A Bronze Guardian
Origin:

- In Greek mythology, Talos was a giant, bronze automaton created by Hephaestus or Daedalus to guard the island of Crete. He was animated by a single vein of molten metal, or "ichor," which served as his lifeblood.

Role in Myth:

- Talos patrolled Crete, protecting it from invaders by hurling stones or heating his body to incinerate enemies. He was ultimately defeated when Medea drained his ichor.

Themes:

- **Protection and Boundaries**: Talos symbolized the guardian archetype, protecting the sacred from external threats.
- **Mortality of the Artificial**: Despite his power, Talos was vulnerable, reflecting the fragility of artificial creations.

4. The Pygmalion Myth: Life from Art
Origin:

- In Ovid's *Metamorphoses*, Pygmalion was a sculptor who fell in love with a statue he created. Moved by his devotion, the goddess Aphrodite brought the statue to life.

Role in Myth:

- This myth emphasizes the power of love and art to transcend boundaries, granting life to the inanimate.

Themes:

- **Art and Creation**: The myth celebrates human creativity and the transformative power of passion.
- **Divine Intervention**: The animation of the statue underscores the collaboration between human effort and divine will.

5. Chinese Jiangshi: The Animated Corpse
Origin:

- The **jiangshi** is a reanimated corpse in Chinese folklore, often described as a "hopping vampire." While not created by human hands, the jiangshi's movement and lifeless origin align it with the golem archetype.

Role in Myth:

- Jiangshi are often created through spells or rituals, brought back to life to fulfill a purpose or as a result of neglecting burial rites.

Themes:

- **Unnatural Animation**: Like the golem, the jiangshi warns against meddling with the natural order of life and death.
- **Control and Chaos**: Jiangshi can become uncontrollable, wreaking havoc on those who disturb them.

6. African Fetishes and Nkisi Figures
Origin:

- Nkisi figures are sacred objects or statues imbued with spiritual power in Central and West African traditions. Though not animated in the physical sense, they are believed to house spirits that can act on behalf of their creators.

Role in Myth:

- These figures are created with rituals and are used for protection, healing, or justice.

Themes:

- **Connection to the Spirit World**: Nkisi figures highlight the belief in a thin boundary between the material and spiritual realms.
- **Responsibility of Creation**: The use of such objects comes with moral and spiritual responsibilities.

7. The Golems of Modern Science Fiction
Origin and Context:

- Modern interpretations of the golem archetype appear in science fiction through robots, artificial intelligence, and androids. Examples include Mary Shelley's *Frankenstein*, Isaac Asimov's robots, and films like *Ex Machina* and *Blade Runner*.

Themes:

- **Humanity's Role as Creator**: These stories explore the ethical dilemmas of creating life, often warning of the dangers of unchecked ambition.
- **Free Will and Agency**: The sentience of these creations raises questions about autonomy and the responsibilities of creators toward their creations.

Universal Themes Across Golem Archetypes
Despite cultural differences, the golem archetype consistently reflects universal concerns and aspirations:

1. **The Power of Creation**: The act of creating life symbolizes human ingenuity and divine inspiration, while also highlighting the responsibilities that come with such power.
2. **Protection and Control**: Golems and their counterparts often serve as protectors, but their potential for destruction reflects the dangers of mismanagement or hubris.
3. **Fragility and Vulnerability**: Whether crafted from clay, bronze, or spirit, golems are inherently fragile, serving as reminders of humanity's own limitations.
4. **Moral and Ethical Boundaries**: Stories of animated beings explore the moral implications of creation, including questions of

free will, agency, and the potential consequences of tampering with natural or divine laws.

Conclusion: The Enduring Relevance of the Golem Archetype

The golem archetype endures across cultures and eras because it resonates with fundamental human concerns: the desire to create, the fear of losing control, and the quest to understand the boundaries of power and responsibility. From the clay golem of Prague to the robotic beings of science fiction, these stories challenge us to reflect on the consequences of our actions and the balance between ambition and humility.

The Gingerbread Golem, as an extension of this archetype, brings these timeless themes into the realm of holiday folklore. Its sweetness and fragility, juxtaposed with its potential for menace, invite us to consider the delicate balance between creation and destruction, joy and caution, that defines the human experience. Through its lens, we find a rich tapestry of mythology that continues to inspire and provoke thought.

Appendix C: Holiday Darkness Around the World
A Collection of Dark Holiday Tales and Myths Across Cultures

While the holiday season is often celebrated for its warmth, light, and joy, many cultures have incorporated elements of darkness into their traditions. These myths and tales serve as reminders of balance, moral lessons, and the inevitability of life's dualities. From the mischievous Krampus to the cautionary Gingerbread Golem, these figures and stories bring depth to the festive season, blending cheer with reflection.

1. Central Europe: Krampus – The Shadow of Saint Nicholas
Origins and Myth

- Krampus is a horned, demonic figure from Alpine folklore who serves as a counterpart to Saint Nicholas. While Nicholas rewards good children with gifts, Krampus punishes the naughty by whipping them with birch branches or dragging them to his lair.
- His name is derived from the German word *krampen*, meaning "claw."

Cultural Role

- Krampus appears during the early December celebrations of *Krampusnacht* (Krampus Night), where costumed figures roam streets, scaring children and adults alike.
- The tale reinforces discipline, ensuring children behave during the festive season.

Themes

- **Duality**: The contrast between Saint Nicholas and Krampus reflects the balance of reward and punishment.

- **Moral Oversight**: Krampus serves as a dark enforcer of good behavior, emphasizing accountability.

2. Iceland: Gryla and the Yule Lads
Origins and Myth

- Gryla is a terrifying ogress in Icelandic folklore who kidnaps and eats misbehaving children during the holiday season. She is said to live in a mountain cave with her lazy husband, Leppalúði, and their mischievous children, the Yule Lads.
- The Yule Lads, originally malevolent pranksters, visit homes during the 13 nights before Christmas, leaving gifts or rotten potatoes depending on children's behavior.

Cultural Role

- Gryla and her family embody the darker side of the Icelandic winter, reminding people to adhere to social norms and moral expectations.
- The Yule Lads have softened over time, now playing a role akin to Santa's elves.

Themes

- **Consequences of Misbehavior**: Gryla's child-eating habit underscores the importance of good conduct.
- **Mischief and Redemption**: The Yule Lads, though once sinister, reflect the complexities of behavior—blending playful and moralistic elements.

3. Germany: The Perchta and Her Dual Nature
Origins and Myth

- Perchta, a goddess of the Alpine regions, has a dual nature: one as a beautiful maiden who rewards hard work and kindness, and the other as a terrifying hag who punishes laziness and deceit.
- During the Twelve Days of Christmas, Perchta visits households. She rewards the diligent with silver coins and punishes the lazy by slitting their bellies and stuffing them with straw.

Cultural Role

- Perchta's myth reinforces the values of hard work, hospitality, and adherence to tradition during the festive season.

Themes

- **Duality of Reward and Punishment**: Perchta's dual form serves as a reminder that behavior has consequences.
- **Cultural Preservation**: Her tale emphasizes the importance of maintaining cultural and familial traditions.

4. Scandinavia: The Yule Cat (Jólakötturinn)
Origins and Myth

- The Yule Cat is a giant, monstrous feline that roams Icelandic villages during Christmas time. It preys on those who have not received new clothes for the holiday season.
- The legend likely originated as a way to motivate workers to complete their wool-spinning tasks before the holidays.

Cultural Role

- The Yule Cat serves as a symbol of industriousness and preparation, linking material rewards (new clothes) with survival and community effort.

Themes

- **Preparation and Responsibility**: The Yule Cat's predatory nature warns against laziness and the dangers of being unprepared.
- **Social Unity**: The tradition ties personal responsibility to communal well-being.

5. Eastern Europe: The Baba Yaga of Winter
Origins and Myth

- Baba Yaga, a prominent figure in Slavic folklore, is a witch who lives in a house on chicken legs in the depths of the forest. Though not explicitly tied to holidays, her winter tales reflect themes of challenge and transformation.
- In some stories, Baba Yaga tests the worthiness of her visitors, offering assistance to those who prove their courage and wit.

Cultural Role

- Baba Yaga's tales are often cautionary, teaching lessons about perseverance, cleverness, and the value of kindness.

Themes

- **Challenge and Growth**: Her trials symbolize personal growth and the rewards of bravery.
- **Ambiguity of Good and Evil**: Baba Yaga's dual nature as both helper and antagonist mirrors life's complexities.

6. Japan: Namahage – The Visiting Oni
Origins and Myth

- Namahage are demon-like figures from Japanese folklore who visit homes during New Year's celebrations, wearing grotesque masks and wielding knives. They admonish children and young adults for laziness or misbehavior.
- The name derives from the Japanese words for "blister" and "peeling," referencing their warning against idleness.

Cultural Role

- Namahage are cultural enforcers, ensuring diligence and respect within the family and community during the new year.

Themes

- **Discipline and Accountability**: Namahage emphasize the value of hard work and respect for elders.
- **Cleansing and Renewal**: Their visits symbolize a fresh start, free from laziness or bad habits.

7. Mexico: La Llorona – A Ghostly Warning
Origins and Myth

- La Llorona ("The Weeping Woman") is a spectral figure in Mexican folklore who roams at night, mourning her drowned children. During the holiday season, her tale serves as a cautionary story to keep children close and safe.

Cultural Role

- La Llorona's presence during the holidays connects themes of loss, morality, and family unity to the festive season.

Themes

- **Grief and Redemption**: Her story highlights the consequences of neglect and the enduring power of maternal love.
- **Protection**: Her myth reinforces the importance of safeguarding family ties.

8. The Gingerbread Golem – A Modern Tale
Origins and Myth

- The Gingerbread Golem, a recent addition to holiday mythology, is a sweet creation brought to life to serve its maker. However, its fragile nature and potential for menace symbolize the duality of holiday traditions.
- Tales of the Gingerbread Golem explore themes of creation, responsibility, and the consequences of neglect.

Cultural Role

- As a holiday figure, the Gingerbread Golem blends whimsy with caution, reminding celebrants of the balance between joy and mindfulness.

Themes

- **Creation and Accountability**: Like other golems, the Gingerbread Golem underscores the ethical considerations of bringing something to life.
- **Impermanence**: Its fragility serves as a metaphor for the transient nature of happiness and the importance of care.

Conclusion: The Dark Side of Celebration

These tales of holiday darkness from around the world highlight humanity's shared need to balance joy with reflection, light with shadow. Whether it's Krampus punishing the naughty, Gryla devouring the lazy, or the Gingerbread Golem embodying the fragility of creation, these myths deepen our understanding of the season. They remind us that even in times of festivity, we must confront our fears, take responsibility for our actions, and honor the complexities of life. By exploring the darkness within holiday traditions, we enrich our celebrations and reconnect with the universal truths that sustain us through the longest nights of the year.

Message from the Author:

I hope you enjoyed this book, I love astrology and knew there was not a book such as this out on the shelf. I love metaphysical items as well. Please check out my other books:

-Life of Government Benefits

-My life of Hell

-My life with Hydrocephalus

-Red Sky

-World Domination:Woman's rule

-World Domination:Woman's Rule 2: The War

-Life and Banishment of Apophis: book 1

-The Kidney Friendly Diet

-The Ultimate Hemp Cookbook

-Creating a Dispensary(legally)

-Cleanliness throughout life: the importance of showering from childhood to adulthood.

-Strong Roots: The Risks of Overcoddling children

-Hemp Horoscopes: Cosmic Insights and Earthly Healing

- Celestial Hemp Navigating the Zodiac: Through the Green Cosmos

-Astrological Hemp: Aligning The Stars with Earth's Ancient Herb

-The Astrological Guide to Hemp: Stars, Signs, and Sacred Leaves

-Green Growth: Innovative Marketing Strategies for your Hemp Products and Dispensary

-Cosmic Cannabis

-Astrological Munchies

-Henry The Hemp

-Zodiacal Roots: The Astrological Soul Of Hemp

- **Green Constellations: Intersection of Hemp and Zodiac**

-Hemp in The Houses: An astrological Adventure Through The Cannabis Galaxy

-Galactic Ganja Guide

Heavenly Hemp
Zodiac Leaves
Doctor Who Astrology
Cannastrology
Stellar Satvias and Cosmic Indicas
Celestial Cannabis: A Zodiac Journey
AstroHerbology: The Sky and The Soil: Volume 1
AstroHerbology:Celestial Cannabis:Volume 2
Cosmic Cannabis Cultivation
The Starry Guide to Herbal Harmony: Volume 1
The Starry Guide to Herbal Harmony: Cannabis Universe: Volume

2

Yugioh Astrology: Astrological Guide to Deck, Duels and more
Nightmare Mansion: Echoes of The Abyss
Nightmare Mansion 2: Legacy of Shadows
Nightmare Mansion 3: Shadows of the Forgotten
Nightmare Mansion 4: Echoes of the Damned
The Life and Banishment of Apophis: Book 2
Nightmare Mansion: Halls of Despair
Healing with Herb: Cannabis and Hydrocephalus
Planetary Pot: Aligning with Astrological Herbs: Volume 1
Fast Track to Freedom: 30 Days to Financial Independence Using AI, Assets, and Agile Hustles
Cosmic Hemp Pathways
How to Become Financially Free in 30 Days: 10,000 Paths to Prosperity
Zodiacal Herbage: Astrological Insights: Volume 1
Nightmare Mansion: Whispers in the Walls
The Daleks Invade Atlantis
Henry the hemp and Hydrocephalus

10X The Kidney Friendly Diet
Cannabis Universe: Adult coloring book

Hemp Astrology: The Healing Power of the Stars

Zodiacal Herbage: Astrological Insights: Cannabis Universe: Volume 2

Planetary Pot: Aligning with Astrological Herbs: Cannabis Universes: Volume 2

Doctor Who Meets the Replicators and SG-1: The Ultimate Battle for Survival

Nightmare Mansion: Curse of the Blood Moon

The Celestial Stoner: A Guide to the Zodiac

Cosmic Pleasures: Sex Toy Astrology for Every Sign

Hydrocephalus Astrology: Navigating the Stars and Healing Waters

Lapis and the Mischievous Chocolate Bar

Celestial Positions: Sexual Astrology for Every Sign

Apophis's Shadow Work Journal: : A Journey of Self-Discovery and Healing

Kinky Cosmos: Sexual Kink Astrology for Every Sign

Digital Cosmos: The Astrological Digimon Compendium

Stellar Seeds: The Cosmic Guide to Growing with Astrology

Apophis's Daily Gratitude Journal

Cat Astrology: Feline Mysteries of the Cosmos

The Cosmic Kama Sutra: An Astrological Guide to Sexual Positions

Unleash Your Potential: A Guided Journal Powered by AI Insights

Whispers of the Enchanted Grove

Cosmic Pleasures: An Astrological Guide to Sexual Kinks

369, 12 Manifestation Journal

Whisper of the nocturne journal(blank journal for writing or drawing)

The Boogey Book
Locked In Reflection: A Chastity Journey Through Locktober
Generating Wealth Quickly:
How to Generate $100,000 in 24 Hours
Star Magic: Harness the Power of the Universe
The Flatulence Chronicles: A Fart Journal for Self-Discovery
The Doctor and The Death Moth
Seize the Day: A Personal Seizure Tracking Journal
The Ultimate Boogeyman Safari: A Journey into the Boogie World and Beyond
Whispers of Samhain: 1,000 Spells of Love, Luck, and Lunar Magic: Samhain Spell Book
Apophis's guides:
Witch's Spellbook Crafting Guide for Halloween
Frost & Flame: The Enchanted Yule Grimoire of 1000 Winter Spells
The Ultimate Boogey Goo Guide & Spooky Activities for Halloween Fun
Harmony of the Scales: A Libra's Spellcraft for Balance and Beauty
The Enchanted Advent: 36 Days of Christmas Wonders

Nightmare Mansion: The Labyrinth of Screams
Harvest of Enchantment: 1,000 Spells of Gratitude, Love, and Fortune for Thanksgiving
The Boogey Chronicles: A Journal of Nightly Encounters and Shadowy Secrets
The 12 Days of Financial Freedom: A Step-by-Step Christmas Countdown to Transform Your Finances
Sigil of the Eternal Spiral Blank Journal
A Christmas Feast: Timeless Recipes for Every Meal
Holiday Stress-Free Solutions: A Survival Guide to Thriving During the Festive Season

Yu-Gi-Oh! Holiday Gifting Mastery: The Ultimate Guide for Fans and Newcomers Alike

Holiday Harmony: A Hydrocephalus Survival Guide for the Festive Season

Celestial Craft: The Witch's Almanac for 2025 – A Cosmic Guide to Manifestations, Moons, and Mystical Events

Doctor Who: The Toymaker's Winter Wonderland

Tulsa King Unveiled: A Thrilling Guide to Stallone's Mafia Masterpiece

Pendulum Craft: A Complete Guide to Crafting and Using Personalized Divination Tools

Nightmare Mansion: Santa's Eternal Eve

Starlight Noel: A Cosmic Journey through Christmas Mysteries

The Dark Architect: Unlocking the Blueprint of Existence

Surviving the Embrace: The Ultimate Guide to Encounters with The Hugging Molly

The Enchanted Codex: Secrets of the Craft for Witches, Wiccans, and Pagans

Harvest of Gratitude: A Complete Thanksgiving Guide

Yuletide Essentials: A Complete Guide to an Authentic and Magical Christmas

Celestial Smokes: A Cosmic Guide to Cigars and Astrology

Living in Balance: A Comprehensive Survival Guide to Thriving with Diabetes Insipidus

Cosmic Symbiosis: The Venom Zodiac Chronicles

The Cursed Paw of Ambition

Cosmic Symbiosis: The Astrological Venom Journal

Celestial Wonders Unfold: A Stargazer's Guide to the Cosmos (2024-2029)

The Ultimate Black Friday Prepper's Guide: Mastering Shopping Strategies and Savings

Cosmic Sales: The Astrological Guide to Black Friday Shopping

Legends of the Corn Mother and Other Harvest Myths

Whispers of the Harvest: The Corn Mother's Journal

The Evergreen Spellbook

The Doctor Meets the Boogeyman

The White Witch of Rose Hall's SpellBook

If you want solar for your home go here: https://www.harborsolar.live/apophisenterprises/

Get Some Tarot cards: https://www.makeplayingcards.com/sell/
apophis-occult-shop

Get some shirts: https://www.bonfire.com/store/apophis-shirt-emporium/

Instagrams:
@apophis_enterprises,
@apophisbookemporium,
@apophisscardshop
Twitter: @apophisenterpr1
 Tiktok:@apophisenterprise
Youtube: @sg1fan23477, @FiresideRetreatKingdom
Hive: @sg1fan23477
CheeLee: @SG1fan23477

Podcast: Apophis Chat Zone: https://open.spotify.com/show/ 5zXbrCLEV2xzCp8ybrfHsk?si=fb4d4fdbdce44dec

Newsletter: https://apophiss-newsletter-27c897.beehiiv.com/

9 798330 603961